G000097445

CRASH RISKS AND SAFETY ISSUES AMONG OLDER DRIVERS

AGING ISSUES, HEALTH AND FINANCIAL ALTERNATIVES

Additional books in this series can be found on Nova's website under the Series tab.

Additional E-books in this series can be found on Nova's website under the E-books tab.

TRANSPORTATION ISSUES, POLICIES AND R&D

Additional books in this series can be found on Nova's website under the Series tab.

Additional E-books in this series can be found on Nova's website under the E-books tab.

AGING ISSUES, HEALTH AND FINANCIAL ALTERNATIVES

CRASH RISKS AND SAFETY ISSUES AMONG OLDER DRIVERS

WILLIAM E. MADSEN
EDITOR

Nova Science Publishers, Inc.
New York

Copyright © 2011 by Nova Science Publishers, Inc.

All rights reserved. No part of this book may be reproduced, stored in a retrieval system or transmitted in any form or by any means: electronic, electrostatic, magnetic, tape, mechanical photocopying, recording or otherwise without the written permission of the Publisher.

For permission to use material from this book please contact us:
Telephone 631-231-7269; Fax 631-231-8175
Web Site: http://www.novapublishers.com

NOTICE TO THE READER

The Publisher has taken reasonable care in the preparation of this book, but makes no expressed or implied warranty of any kind and assumes no responsibility for any errors or omissions. No liability is assumed for incidental or consequential damages in connection with or arising out of information contained in this book. The Publisher shall not be liable for any special, consequential, or exemplary damages resulting, in whole or in part, from the readers' use of, or reliance upon, this material. Any parts of this book based on government reports are so indicated and copyright is claimed for those parts to the extent applicable to compilations of such works.

Independent verification should be sought for any data, advice or recommendations contained in this book. In addition, no responsibility is assumed by the publisher for any injury and/or damage to persons or property arising from any methods, products, instructions, ideas or otherwise contained in this publication.

This publication is designed to provide accurate and authoritative information with regard to the subject matter covered herein. It is sold with the clear understanding that the Publisher is not engaged in rendering legal or any other professional services. If legal or any other expert assistance is required, the services of a competent person should be sought. FROM A DECLARATION OF PARTICIPANTS JOINTLY ADOPTED BY A COMMITTEE OF THE AMERICAN BAR ASSOCIATION AND A COMMITTEE OF PUBLISHERS.

Additional color graphics may be available in the e-book version of this book.

LIBRARY OF CONGRESS CATALOGING-IN-PUBLICATION DATA

Crash risks and safety issues among older drivers / editor, William E. Madsen.
     p. cm.
   Includes index.
   ISBN 978-1-61209-348-2 (hardcover)
   1. Older automobile drivers. 2. Traffic safety. 3. Traffic accidents--Risk assessment. I. Madsen, William E.
   HE5620.A24C73 2010
   363.12'52--dc22
                              2010051526
ISBN 9789-1-61209-348-2

Published by Nova Science Publishers, Inc. ✢ *New York*

CONTENTS

PREFACE

This new book examines driver, vehicle, roadway and environmental characteristics associated with increased crash involvement by older drivers. Project activities were designed to prioritize the situations causing problems for older drivers based on the magnitude of the crash problem, older driver's degree of over-representation, the likelihood of serious injury, or other criteria of interest. The resulting list of the most problematic situations frame further discussions of how age-related functional decline can mediate increased crash risk for older drivers, and hopefully, point to potential countermeasures for lowering this risk.

Chapter 1- This chapter presents findings from analyses that highlight driver, vehicle, roadway and environmental characteristics associated with increased crash involvement by older drivers. Fatality Analysis Reporting System (FARS) and National Automotive Sampling System (NASS)/General Estimates System (GES) data from 2002 through 2006 were included in the study. The findings will be useful in developing countermeasures for lowering this risk.

The data were analyzed using two different approaches. Descriptive analyses of single- vehicle and two-vehicle crashes, using FARS and GES data, identified situations in which older drivers were overrepresented compared to younger drivers. A more in-depth, "induced exposure" analysis was undertaken for the two-vehicle crashes in the databases to compare the ratios of at-fault to not-at-fault drivers within age groups. This technique compared the ratios of at-fault to not-at-fault drivers within age groups, producing a crash involvement ratio (CIR) that signifies the degree of over- or under-involvement of each group with respect to particular risk factors. This approach uses each group as its own control, thus taking into account differences in driving exposure across age groups with respect to a particular factor such as driving at nighttime, or on Interstate highways.

Chapter 2- As people age, their physical, visual, and cognitive abilities may decline, making it more difficult for them to drive safely. Older drivers are also more likely to suffer injuries or die in crashes than drivers in other age groups (see fig.). These safety issues will increase in significance because older adults represent the fastest- growing U.S. population segment.

GAO examined (1) what the federal government has done to promote practices to make roads safer for older drivers and the extent to which states have implemented those practices, (2) the extent to which states assess the fitness of older drivers and what support the federal government has provided, and (3) what initiatives selected states have implemented to improve the safety of older drivers. To conduct this study, GAO surveyed 51 state departments of transportation (DOT), visited six states, and interviewed federal transportation officials.

In: Crash Risks and Safety Issues Among... ISBN: 978-1-61209-348-2
Editor: William E. Madsen © 2011 Nova Science Publishers, Inc.

Chapter 1

IDENTIFYING BEHAVIORS AND SITUATIONS ASSOCIATED WITH INCREASED CRASH RISK FOR OLDER DRIVERS

National Highway Traffic Safety Administration

EXECUTIVE SUMMARY

This report presents findings from analyses that highlight driver, vehicle, roadway and environmental characteristics associated with increased crash involvement by older drivers. Fatality Analysis Reporting System (FARS) and National Automotive Sampling System (NASS)/General Estimates System (GES) data from 2002 through 2006 were included in the study. The findings will be useful in developing countermeasures for lowering this risk.

The data were analyzed using two different approaches. Descriptive analyses of single- vehicle and two-vehicle crashes, using FARS and GES data, identified situations in which older drivers were overrepresented compared to younger drivers. A more in-depth, "induced exposure" analysis was undertaken for the two-vehicle crashes in the databases to compare the ratios of at-fault to not-at-fault drivers within age groups. This technique compared the ratios of at-fault to not-at-fault drivers within age groups, producing a crash involvement ratio (CIR) that signifies the degree of over- or under-involvement of each group with respect to particular risk factors. This approach uses each group as its own control, thus taking into account differences in driving exposure across age groups with respect to a particular factor such as driving at nighttime, or on Interstate highways.

METHODS

Development of Data Files

The 2002-2006 FARS and GES crash data were analyzed to identify factors contributing to older driver crashes. For both the FARS and GES data, the analyses were restricted to single- and two-vehicle crashes involving passenger cars, sport utility vehicles, light vans, pickups, and other light trucks.

Two-vehicle crashes included in the induced exposure analyses were those in which *both vehicles* were one of these body types and only one of the drivers had a contributing factor or moving violation. Crashes in which both drivers had contributing factors, or in which neither was identified with a contributing factor, were excluded from the analysis (see Reinfurt et al., 2000). Non-performance-related violations (e.g., driving with a suspended or revoked license) were not considered in determining fault. Following this approach, *88.5%* of the two-vehicle crashes involving eligible vehicle types in the FARS data and *52%* of those in the GES data were coded as having one at-fault and one not-at-fault driver.

Data Analysis

Descriptive analyses of single-vehicle and two-vehicle crashes highlighted the factors that most strongly characterize older driver crashes. Crosstabulations based on age and crash descriptors focused on identifying vehicle maneuvers, crash types or situations where older drivers were over-represented compared to other age groups. The age groups of interest in these analyses were *60 to 69, 70 to 79,* and *80 and older.*

For two-vehicle crashes, an additional set of analyses compared at-fault versus not-atfault crash involvement ratios across driver age categories. This approach controls for potentially different exposure levels across different age groups, and is useful for pinpointing situations that pose the greatest risks to older drivers. Analysis results include full data tables and graphs showing the calculated crash involvement ratio (CIR) values illustrate which factors were most problematic for drivers of different ages.

RESULTS

The descriptive analyses of the FARS and GES data are presented in a series of tables that present crash rates according to characteristics of the driver, vehicle, roadway and environment, the crash, and the condition of the driver. Older drivers were overrepresented in a variety of types of crashes; however, in most situations the overrepresentation was not evident in drivers younger than 70. Drivers 60 and older were less likely than other drivers to be involved in alcohol-related, speed-related, or nighttime-related crashes.

Drivers 60 to 69 had crash rates similar to those of middle-aged drivers under most conditions, although their crash risk was elevated during daylight hours (which may reflect this group's avoidance of night driving) and at intersections. Left turns in general proved risky for older drivers. In two-vehicle crashes, those 60 and older were more likely to be the struck (as opposed to the striking) vehicle, to be involved in angle crashes, and to have received citations for failure to yield. In single-vehicle crashes, drivers 60 and older were more likely to have been alone in the vehicle, and to crash into a parked car and were less likely to have made a maneuver to avoid the collision. Drivers 70 and older had elevated risk levels under additional conditions including driveways, alleys, and at intersections controlled by stop or yield signs.

As expected, the oldest group, drivers 80 and older, were overrepresented in crashes. This group generally differed from those 70 to 79 more in terms of degree of risk elevation, than in number of conditions under which risk was elevated. This was particularly the case under conditions that required navigating complex situations such as intersections, left turns, and reacting to an imminent crash.

The induced exposure analyses added further insight to these findings by providing the ratio of at-fault to not-at-fault drivers (the crash involvement ratio, or CIR) for various crash types for each age group. Values lower than 1.0 indicate lower than average rates of at-fault crashes, and higher than 1.0 represent higher at-fault rates. Overall, FARS data indicate that drivers 60 to 69 had a CIR of 0.75, indicating a below-average risk of being found at fault in a crash. This risk increased to 1.75 for drivers 70 to 79, and to 4.0 for those 80 and older.

Results based on GES data differed in that the increase in CIR with age was less extreme. The CIR for the 60-to-69 age group was similar to that for the FARS data at 0.73. The values for the two older groups were 1.14 for drivers 70 to 79 and 1.91 for those 80 and older. While these scores are higher than average, they are well below those based on the FARS data. The results suggest that at least some of the increase in crash risk seen in the FARS analyses may result from older adults' increased risk of dying in a crash. Thus, the degree of discrepancy may vary with crash type; for example, side impact crash analyses may be more impacted by older driver frailty than rear-end crashes.

Both the FARS and GES analyses demonstrate that drivers 60 to 69 managed most traffic situations nearly as well as their middle-aged counterparts, with only slight elevations in CIRs when navigating intersections controlled by flashing lights and when turning left at intersections with traffic signals. CIRs increased somewhat for drivers 70 to 79 under complex driving conditions such as navigating higher speed, multiple lane roadways, particularly at junctions. While the 70- to 79-year-olds managed most driving tasks nearly as well as their 60- to 69-year-old counterparts, the oldest group generally had substantially higher CIRs under a variety of conditions, indicating higher proportions of at-fault crashes. Driving alone or with one passenger was associated with increased at-fault crashes with increasing age.

INTRODUCTION AND BACKGROUND

This report reviews published literature and analyzes the most recent Fatality Analysis Reporting System (FARS) and National Automotive Sampling System (NAS S)/General Estimates System (GES) data to identify specific driving behaviors (performance errors), and combinations of driver, vehicle, and roadway/environmental characteristics associated with increased crash involvement by older drivers. These project activities were designed to prioritize the situations causing problems for older drivers based on the magnitude of the crash problem, older drivers' degree of over-representation, the likelihood of serious injury, or other criteria of interest. The resulting list of the most problematic situations will frame the later discussion of how age-related functional decline can mediate increased crash risk for older drivers and, hopefully, point to potential countermeasures for lowering this risk.

Two analytic approaches were undertaken. The first approach was to carry out separate descriptive analyses of single-vehicle and two-vehicle crashes, looking for situations where older drivers were overrepresented compared to younger drivers. This relied on crosstabulations of FARS and GES data for the 5-year period 2002-2006. A more in-depth, "induced exposure" analysis was undertaken for the two-vehicle crashes. This technique compared the ratios of at- fault to not-at-fault drivers within age groups, producing a crash involvement ratio (CIR) that signifies the degree of over- or under-involvement of each group with respect to particular risk factors. While feasible only with large data sets, this approach is notable in that it seeks to use each group as its own control, thus taking into account differences in driving exposure across age groups with respect to a particular factor such as driving at nighttime, or on Interstate highways.

Previous work in this area has highlighted a number of older driver difficulties related to specific traffic maneuvers and roadway conditions. Two studies in particular served as models for the current effort. One was an analysis by Staplin and Lyles (1991) that used 1986-1988 Michigan crash data to examine five specific vehicle maneuver patterns: merging and weaving on limited-access highways, lane changes on limited-access highways, left turns against traffic, crossing-gap-acceptance maneuvers, and overtaking on two-lane rural roadways. A sample table from the analysis results for one of these maneuvers is shown below, where Driver 1 is the at- fault driver and Driver 2 the not-at-fault driver in two-vehicle crashes:

| Driver 1 | Driver 2 Age[1] | | | | |
Age	≤26	27-55	56-75	76-98	Totals
≤26	232 (28.5)	501 (61.5)	79 (9.7)	3 (0.4)	815 (32.5)
27-55	380 (27.1)	872 (62.2)	139 (9.9)	11 (0.8)	1,402 (55.9)
56-75	65 (24.3)	177 (66.3)	24 (9.0)	1 (0.4)	267 (10.7)
76-98	5 (22.7)	16 (72.7)	1 (4.5)	0 (0.0)	22 (0.9)
Totals	682 (27.2)	1,566 (62.5)	243 (9.7)	15 (0.6)	2,506

[1] Number of accidents (row percentage)
From Staplin and Lyles (1991).

Based on the ratio of at-fault to not-at-fault drivers in each age category, the authors concluded that drivers 76 and older were overrepresented in crashes associated with this specific type of maneuver (involvement ratio =

22/15 = 1.47). Using similarly formatted Pennsylvania crash data, the authors also examined specific operator performance failure categories, showing, for example, that adults 76 and older were much more likely to be cited for making improper exits from a roadway, proceeding without clearance after stopping at an intersection, improper turning, and careless lane changes (Staplin and Lyles, 1991).

The second study that helped guide the current effort was an analysis of North Carolina, FARS, and GES crash data carried out by Reinfurt, Stewart, Stutts, and Rodgman (2000). The goal of this study was to identify driver maneuvers, crash types, or situations that account for an increasing share of at-fault crashes as drivers age. Fault status was determined based on contributing factors cited by the investigating officer. Specifically, in two-vehicle crashes, if one driver was cited for one or more contributing factors and the other driver was not cited for any contributing factors, the first driver was deemed at-fault in the crash. Logistic models were then developed to examine factors associated with being at-fault in a particular type of crash. For example, it was found that with increasing age, drivers were more likely to be at-fault in left-turn crashes involving frontal and right-side impact, and when the traffic control was a stop or yield sign versus a traffic signal.

Others have also used induced exposure techniques to examine the safety of older drivers. Garber and Srinivasan (1991) used an approach similar to Staplin and Lyles (1991) to examine characteristics of elderly driver intersection crashes in Virginia. Variables examined included age, gender, location, type of collision, vehicle maneuver, driver action, type of intersection, and traffic control. The significance of computed crash involvement ratios was tested using t-tests. Results showed older drivers significantly more likely to be involved in intersection crashes in both urban and rural areas, with higher rates of angle, sideswipe, and head-on collision types; left turn maneuvers; and stop sign control intersections. Involvement ratios were higher for female than male drivers.

More recently, Chandraratna and Stamatiadis (2003) used induced exposure to study problem driving maneuvers of older drivers. Of particular relevance methodologically to the current effort, the authors found that including more than two drivers in multi-vehicle crashes did not significantly affect the distribution of not-at-fault driver age (i.e., the distribution of exposed drivers). Consequently, in their study using 1995-1999 Kentucky crash data, the authors only used the first two drivers in multi-vehicle crashes for classifying at-fault versus not-at-fault drivers. Their results showed that older drivers, and especially female older drivers, were significantly more likely to be involved in crashes involving left turns against oncoming traffic, high-speed lane changes, and gap acceptance when crossing a non-limited access highway.

There are numerous other studies, most of a more descriptive nature, that examine the characteristics of older driver crashes compared to those of younger or middle-age drivers. Several of the most recent and relevant are briefly summarized below.

- Mayhew, Simpson, and Ferguson (2006) published a comprehensive review of the literature on the topic of high-risk conditions and locations for older driver crashes. More recent study results were summarized with respect to environmental and weather conditions, illness and medical conditions, alcohol, driving errors, responsibility, crash characteristics, and intersection crashes. Older drivers were found more likely to crash at intersections, especially when making a left turn and as a result of failing to yield the right-of-way, disregarding the traffic signal, or committing some other traffic violation. The authors concluded that *"the extent to which the distinctive characteristics of senior drivers' crashes may be due to changing travel patterns associated with aging, or physical or cognitive impairments related to the aging process, is unclear. Further research is needed to understand the pre-crash circumstances of older drivers' intersection crashes."*

- Braitman, Kirley, Ferguson and Chaudhary (2007) interviewed older drivers involved in recent intersection crashes in Connecticut and took photos of the intersections to obtain additional detail on factors contributing to the crashes. The study involved two samples of at-fault older drivers (ages 70 to 79 and 80 and older) and a comparison sample of at-fault drivers 35 to 54 years old. Findings were especially enlightening with regard to failure to yield crashes, where there were differences even between the two oldest groups of drivers. Drivers ages 70 to 79 were more likely to make errors in gap acceptance, while drivers 80 and older were more likely to fail to see or detect an approaching vehicle.

- A number of recent Australian studies (cf. Langford and Koppel, 2006; Langford, Koppel, Andrea, & Fildes, 2006; and Oxley, Fildes, Corben, & Langford, 2006) have focused on older driver crash characteristics, potential contributing factors, and crash reduction measures. Based on an analysis of 1996-1999 fatal Australian crash data, older adults were twice as likely to be involved in right turn crashes (equivalent to left turn crashes in the United States) into the paths of oncoming vehicles; twice as likely to be involved in right-angle collisions when traveling through intersections; and five times as likely to be involved in perpendicular path collisions at intersections where the older drivers were making right turns (left turns in the United States). And based on Tasmania crash data, the odds of being at fault in a multi-vehicle non-intersection crash were 1.78, compared to 3.55 for a multi-vehicle intersection crash. Countermeasures were addressed in all the studies, and included roadway design measures, traffic control measures (including traffic circles and speed lowering measures), training in route selection, and newer cars.

- McGwin and Brown (1999) analyzed a single year of Alabama crash data, combined with National Household Travel Survey licensed driver and vehicle-miles-traveled data, to describe characteristics of older versus younger and middle-age driver crashes that point to factors that can be examined in the current study. The authors also presented a good review of relevant literature, including studies using induced exposure techniques, and discussed functional declines and other risk factors contributing to older driver crashes.

These and other studies were helpful in guiding the current data analysis task and in interpreting the results with respect to developing the most relevant taxonomy of older driver crash characteristics and risk factors. A discussion of analysis methods precedes the results of the descriptive and induced exposure analyses of older drivers' crash experience.

METHOD

Development of Data Files

The current examination of factors contributing to older driver crashes used 2002-2006 FARS and GES crash data. Consideration was given to using Crashworthiness Data System (CD S) data; however, the CDS is based on a much smaller number of actual crashes (less than 5,000 per year, compared to some 56,000 for the GES). For example, a preliminary analysis of 2006 CDS data revealed only three reported crashes involving an older drivers merging in traffic. Although the raw CDS data are weighted to reflect national crash numbers, such small counts can lead to unstable estimates if used in the sort of finely stratified analysis planned for the current project.

For both the FARS and GES data, the data analysis files developed for use in the project were restricted to single- and two-vehicle crashes involving the following vehicle types:

- passenger cars;
- sport utility vehicles;
- light vans;
- pickups; and
- other light trucks (gross vehicle weight rating <10,000 lbs.).

In order for a two-vehicle crash to be included in the database, *both vehicles* needed to be one of these body types. This analysis *excluded* crashes involving large trucks, motorcycles, pedestrians and bicyclists, as well as crashes involving more than two vehicles.

A second step in the preparation of the study files was the assignment of fault or responsibility for the crash. Neither the FARS nor the GES data contains a variable indicating driver fault. In the Reinfurt et al. (2000) study using FARS and GES crash data, fault was determined based on a driver's contributing factors and/or violations. Specifically, in two- vehicle crashes, a driver was deemed at-fault in the crash if the driver had one or more contributing factors or moving violations, and the other driver had no identified contributing factors or moving violations. Crashes in which both drivers had contributing factors, or in which neither driver was identified with a contributing factor, were excluded from the analysis. For the current study, this same approach was followed for assigning fault to drivers involved in fatal two-vehicle crashes, using the FARS variables *Related Factors – Driver Level (P22)* and *Violations Charged (P21)*. As before, non-performance-related factors or violations – such as "driving with a suspended or revoked license," "obscured vision," and "defective vehicle equipment" – were not considered in determining a driver's fault. Following this approach, *88.5%* of the two-vehicle crashes involving eligible vehicle types in the FARS data were coded as having one at-fault and one not-at-fault driver.

For a listing of the variables and variable levels used in determining fault for the FARS data cases, see Appendix A. Fault definition rules are presented in Appendix B.

Table 1. Eligible single- and two-vehicle crashes for FARS and GES study files

Crash Type and Fault Status	2002-2006 FARS	2002-2006 GES	
		Unweighted	Weighted
Single-vehicle	72,847	69,689	7,860,000
Two-vehicle, only one driver at-fault	37,090	62,090	8,112,000
Two-vehicle, neither driver at fault	1,624	45,062	6,975,000
Two-vehicle, both drivers at fault	3,195	4,857	567,000
Two-vehicle, without regard to fault	41,909	112,009	15,654,000

Applying this approach to the GES data was less successful. While there still exists a similar variable (*Critical Event, Precrash 2*) describing contributing pre-crash events in the GES data, this variable has undergone substantial revisions since utilized by Reinfurt et al.; and, documentation for data collectors clearly states that culpability should not be considered a factor in determining pre-crash vehicle events. Indeed, when crosstabulating a potential grouping of the *Critical Event, Precrash 2* variable by violation charged, there was a high level of "disagreement" between this variable and violation charged.

Consequently, a decision was made to assign fault status in the GES datafile based purely on the violation variable (*Violation Charged, D02*). The following variable levels were considered indicative of fault: *alcohol, drugs, speeding, reckless driving, failure to yield right-of- way, running a traffic signal or stop sign, violation charged-no details*, and *other violation*. It should be noted that neither "driving with a suspended or revoked license" nor "hit-and-run" were used to assign fault, along with "unknown if charged" and "not reported." It is likely that driver violations more often go unreported than contributing factors, and a possible bias in officers citing (older) drivers for violation may be acknowledged. Notwithstanding these limitations, the present approach allowed *52%* of eligible two-vehicle crashes to be coded as one driver at fault and one not-at-fault for use in the induced exposure analyses in GES. At the same time, the severe restrictions on determining fault for crashes in the GES datafile led to a decision to generate the descriptive two-vehicle crash statistics on *all* crashes involving eligible vehicle types, without regard to fault status.

The total number of crashes utilized in the FARS data analyses was 109,937 (72,847 single-vehicle plus 37,090 two-vehicle, where one vehicle was identified at fault). For the GES data analysis, the raw number of crashes available for analysis was 181,698 (69,689 single- vehicle and 112,009 two-vehicle, without regard to fault status), which translated into 23.5 million weighted crashes. Table 1 shows the distribution of single- and two-vehicle crashes involving eligible study vehicles, and their at-fault status, for both the FARS and GES datafiles.

Data Analysis

As noted, separate analyses were carried out on single-vehicle and two-vehicle crashes, to identify the factors that most strongly characterize older driver crashes. For the crosstabulations involving age and other crash descriptors, the focus was on identifying specific vehicle maneuvers and crash types or situations where older drivers are over-represented compared to middle-aged drivers, or where there is a pattern of increased involvement with age. Driver gender was examined as a potential mediating variable, along with other situational variables such as light condition, number of travel lanes, and speed limit. These descriptive analyses are important in that they identify crash scenarios that comprise the biggest proportion of the older driver crash "problem." The age groups included in these analyses were: *60 to 69, 70 to 79, and 80 and older.*

Table 2. Sample induced exposure table for a specified a two-vehicle crash situation

Driver 1 Age (at fault)	Driver2 Age (not-at-fault)								
	<20	20-29	30-39	40-49	50-59	60-69	70-79	80+	Total
<20									$D1_a$
20-29									$D1_b$
30-39									$D1_c$
40-49									$D1_d$
50-59									$D1_e$
60-69									$D1_f$
70-79									$D1_g$
80+									$D1_h$
Total	$D2_a$	$D2_b$	$D2_c$	$D2_d$	$D2_e$	$D2_f$	$D2_g$	$D2_h$	Total

For two-vehicle crashes, an additional set of analyses compared at-fault versus not-at-fault crash involvement ratios across driver age categories, for a particular crash type or crash situation. As previously described, this approach, based on the concept of *induced exposure*, takes into account potentially different exposure levels across different age groups, and is therefore especially useful for pinpointing situations that pose the greatest risks to older drivers. The relative involvement of drivers in at-fault, versus not-at-fault, crashes is expressed as a crash involvement ratio (CIR).

The following eight categories of driver age were used in the induced exposure analyses: *<20, 20-29, 30-39, 40-49, 50-59, 60-69, 70-79,* and *80+.* This differed from the mid-decade grouping initially proposed, as the relatively small number of drivers in the 85-and-older category could hinder valid comparisons in some of the less common crash situations (e.g., changing lanes or merging on freeways).

Table 2 shows the typical table layout for the induced exposure analyses, where $D1_a$ is the number of drivers under 20 who were identified at-fault in the particular two-vehicle crash situation being examined, and $D2_a$ the number of identified not-at-fault drivers under 20. The at-fault CIR for drivers under age 20 is then $D1_a /D2_a$. Similar ratios can be calculated for the other age groups, using row and column totals to indicate which groups are over- (or under-) represented in the particular crash situation under study.

Analysis results include full data tables (as shown below), which were generated to check for adequate sample sizes. Graphs showing the calculated CIR values illustrate which situations and (combinations of) factors were most problematic for drivers of different ages. It may be noted that significance testing on the observed differences was *not* performed, as these descriptive analyses were not initiated with any particular set of hypotheses in mind.

RESULTS OF FARS DATA ANALYSIS

Characteristics of Older Driver Fatal Crashes

Descriptive results based on the combined 2002-2006 FARS data have been organized according to *driver, vehicle, roadway/environmental, crash characteristic,* and *contributing factors* variables (Tables 3-7, respectively). For each of the tables, results are presented separately for single-vehicle and two-vehicle crashes. The displayed values represent the percentages of all drivers/crashes for the particular age group (i.e., column percents), although to be concise, not all levels of a variable are presented; "other" and "unknown" levels were always omitted, as were other variable levels having small percentages or little relevance to the topic. As a result, the sum of the percentages for a particular variable and age group is typically slightly less than 100%.

The following material includes a bullet list to summarize key findings with respect to each of the tables. As noted earlier, *both exposure and "increased risk" can contribute to any observed over- or under-representation* in these descriptive data.

Driver Characteristics

- Female older drivers were slightly overrepresented, especially in single-vehicle fatal crashes; however, this may be due at least in part to demographic changes with age.
- Alcohol was much less likely to play a role in older driver crashes, and this likelihood decreased with age.
- Older drivers were slightly more likely than younger drivers to be carrying just one passenger when involved in a two-vehicle fatal crash (i.e., two occupants in the vehicle). They were much less likely to be carrying two or more passengers (three+ vehicle occupants). Conversely, they were more likely to be driving alone, especially when involved in a single-vehicle crash.

Table 3. 2002-2006 FARS descriptive results – driver characteristics1

Driver Characteristics	Two-Vehicle Crashes				Single-Vehicle Crashes			
	60-69	70-79	80+	All ages	60-69	70-79	80+	All ages
Gender								
Male	64.70	62.58	65.08	65.97	71.69	71.34	68.74	74.66
Female	35.30	37.42	34.92	33.70	28.31	28.63	31.15	24.82
Alcohol								
No alcohol	60.65	62.83	64.98	54.62	43.56	51.13	55.33	29.16
Yes alcohol	3.45	2.16	1.00	9.44	13.80	5.76	1.96	30.74
Not reported	35.90	35.02	34.02	35.93	42.63	43.10	42.72	40.10

Table 3. (Continued)

Driver Characteristics	Two-Vehicle Crashes				Single-Vehicle Crashes			
	60-69	70-79	80+	All ages	60-69	70-79	80+	All ages
Occupants								
One	59.67	58.41	63.97	57.96	72.17	70.44	74.44	56.66
Two	30.09	34.37	32.06	25.97	19.75	24.23	22.86	23.98
Three+	10.24	7.23	3.97	15.00	8.08	5.33	2.70	19.35

[1] Percentages of drivers in each age category (column percents); overall includes all age groups.

Vehicle Characteristics

- Compared to the overall population of drivers involved in two-vehicle fatal crashes, drivers 70 and older (but not those 60 to 69), were more likely to be driving standard automobiles (or automobile derivatives), and less likely to be driving utility vehicles or light trucks. The same trend holds with respect to single-vehicle crashes, although the pattern is less pronounced and more characteristic of the 80-and-older driver group.
- Drivers in the 60-to-69 and 70-to-79 age groups were slightly more likely to be driving a recent model vehicle, while those 80 and older were more likely to be driving vehicles that were 10 years old or older.

Table 4. 2002-2006 FARS descriptive results – vehicle characteristics

Vehicle Characteristics	Two-Vehicle Crashes				Single-Vehicle Crashes			
	60-69	70-79	80+	All ages	60-69	70-79	80+	All ages
Body Type								
Automobile/deriv	52.77	70.71	81.22	54.40	42.99	56.46	71.62	52.29
Utility vehicle	12.45	6.01	3.67	14.49	18.88	11.67	7.43	18.64
Van-based lt truck	10.26	7.99	4.80	7.96	9.33	7.85	5.35	5.23
Light truck	24.25	15.20	10.24	22.89	28.73	23.98	15.60	23.74
Vehicle Age								
<5 years	34.70	32.66	25.31	31.77	33.71	33.06	27.75	29.38
5-9 years	31.87	30.56	31.43	32.68	30.41	28.92	29.02	32.50
10+ years	33.14	36.66	43.27	35.38	35.74	37.85	42.89	37.89

Roadway/Environmental Characteristics

- Two-vehicle older driver fatal crashes were less likely to occur on Interstates (70+), and more likely to occur on U.S. highways. They were also slightly less likely to occur on county roads. Single-vehicle older driver fatal crashes were even more underrepresented on county roads, while becoming overrepresented on municipal roadways. In addition, drivers 60 to 69 were slightly overrepresented in fatal single-vehicle crashes on Interstates, while those 80 and older were underrepresented. In general, however, older drivers' fatal crash locations were not much different from that of the overall driving population.

- With increasing age, older drivers' single- and two-vehicle crashes were increasingly likely to occur in urban areas, although the majority of their fatal crashes still occurred on rural roadways.

- Starting at age 70, older drivers in two-vehicle crashes were especially likely to crash at intersections, with the likelihood of an intersection crash strongly associated with increasing age. Over half of all fatal two-vehicle crashes involving drivers 70+ occurred at intersections. Older adults were also overrepresented in two-vehicle crashes at driveway or alley junctions, but not at interchange junctions.

- Drivers 70+ were overrepresented in single-vehicle fatal crashes at roadway and driveway/alley intersections; and increasingly with age, drivers 60+ were overrepresented in single-vehicle crashes at railroad crossing locations.

- Drivers 80 and older were overrepresented in single- and two-vehicle crashes on lower speed roadways, and underrepresented in crashes on higher speed roadways. Still, even for drivers in this oldest age group, nearly half of fatal two-vehicle and single-vehicle crashes occur on roadways with speed limits greater than 45 mph.

- Older drivers were less likely to crash while negotiating a curve in the roadway (a factor likely related to their reduced likelihood of speeding).

Table 5. 2002-2006 FARS descriptive results – roadway and environmental characteristics

Roadway Characteristics	Two-Vehicle Crashes				Single-Vehicle Crashes			
	60-69	70-79	80+	All ages	60-69	70-79	80+	All ages
Route signing								
Interstate	7.17	4.66	2.81	7.18	18.95	16.31	10.25	14.83
U.S. highway	23.78	25.96	24.91	21.10	13.98	13.65	11.86	11.02
State highway	35.75	37.05	34.07	34.84	27.41	26.54	29.76	25.54
County road	15.64	14.03	14.16	16.51	21.81	20.63	21.07	26.93
Township	2.81	3.21	3.94	3.43	4.38	5.62	6.33	5.78
Municipality	10.45	10.91	15.79	12.09	7.98	11.78	15.72	10.16
Rural/urban roadway								
Rural	61.93	58.44	49.74	58.02	71.37	67.30	60.44	67.10
Urban	36.57	39.84	48.47	40.49	27.05	30.65	37.30	31.40
Relation to junction								
Non-junction	52.49	39.32	27.17	53.73	88.60	85.92	81.58	89.53
Intersection/int-rel	41.25	51.82	62.21	40.08	5.58	7.63	10.25	5.37
Driveway/alley	2.00	2.96	3.89	1.73	0.40	0.79	1.04	0.39
Interchange- related	2.45	2.47	2.31	2.44	2.60	1.84	2.25	2.65
Railroad crossing	0.02	0.02	0.00	0.03	2.10	3.24	3.80	1.32
Number lanes								
1-2	76.60	75.20	72.03	75.43	83.97	84.99	86.29	84.67
3-4	19.81	21.06	23.73	20.58	13.61	12.28	11.51	12.69
5+	2.81	2.74	2.79	2.99	1.45	1.58	1.04	1.57
Speed limit								
≤ 35 mph	13.76	14.89	21.04	14.98	17.42	20.74	28.16	18.92
40-45 mph	22.69	25.29	28.30	23.18	14.20	15.52	15.32	17.28
50-60 mph	46.82	45.73	38.66	46.23	39.73	37.31	35.35	40.71
65+ mph	15.31	12.13	9.99	14.13	26.41	23.55	16.47	20.51
Roadway alignm'nt								
Straight	81.67	84.87	89.68	81.57	66.97	71.01	70.18	61.39
Curve	17.97	14.75	9.64	18.06	32.53	28.63	29.02	37.94
Traffic Control								
None	60.51	51.68	44.21	61.59	88.80	87.61	84.23	89.25
Signal (all)	12.26	15.00	16.52	12.67	1.61	2.02	3.06	1.47
Stop sign	22.68	28.82	35.88	21.27	2.00	2.48	4.84	2.05
Yield sign	0.72	1.00	0.90	0.69	--	--	--	--
Light Condition								
Daylight	74.27	82.43	88.30	63.39	66.64	76.88	81.98	40.00

Table 5. (Continued)

Roadway Characteristics	Two-Vehicle Crashes				Single-Vehicle Crashes			
	60-69	70-79	80+	All ages	60-69	70-79	80+	All ages
Dark	14.97	9.07	5.20	20.10	22.46	14.40	10.31	41.65
Dark, lighted	6.97	5.19	3.97	12.11	6.48	4.97	4.55	13.86
Dawn	1.41	0.76	0.40	1.85	2.08	1.26	0.81	2.07
Dusk	2.24	2.41	1.98	2.44	2.03	1.76	1.84	1.79
Weather								
Normal	85.53	87.93	89.13	85.54	86.45	88.08	89.29	87.74
Rain	9.55	8.60	8.36	9.72	8.08	7.42	6.56	7.78
Sleet/snow/fog/etc	4.83	3.31	2.26	4.55	4.99	3.86	3.11	3.68

- While drivers 70 and older were somewhat overrepresented in two-vehicle crashes at traffic signal locations, they were much more overrepresented in two-vehicle crashes at stop sign locations. Over a third of fatal two-vehicle crashes involving drivers 80 and older occurred at stop sign locations – twice the percentage as at signal locations.
- All age groups of older drivers were overrepresented in daylight fatal crashes; this percentage increased substantially with age for both single- and two-vehicle crashes.
- Older people were increasingly less likely to be driving the striking vehicles in two- vehicle crashes, and more likely to be driving the struck vehicles.

Crash Characteristics

- Older drivers were less likely to be involved in non-collision single-vehicle fatal crashes, such as rollovers, and more likely to strike fixed objects, other parked or stopped vehicles, and non-fixed objects. This effect increased with age.
- In two-vehicle fatal crashes, older drivers were more likely to be driving the struck, as opposed to the striking vehicles. The effect increased with age.
- Older drivers were more likely to be struck in the side, particularly the left side, in two- vehicle crashes; both left- and right-side impacts increased sharply with age. In single- vehicle fatal crashes, they are increasingly more likely to experience frontal impact.

- After age 70, drivers were overrepresented in front-to-side collisions with vehicles traveling on perpendicular paths, and underrepresented in head-on collisions. Both left- and right-side initial impacts with other vehicles increased sharply with driver age.
- By far, the maneuver posing greatest problems for older drivers was the left turn. While drivers 60 to 69 were only slightly overrepresented in crashes involving left turns, the percentage doubled to 20% for drivers 70 to 79, and increased to 32% for drivers 80 and older. Right turns and U-turns became more problematic as drivers aged, but represented only a small proportion of fatal crashes.
- Older drivers involved in single-vehicle fatal crashes were somewhat more likely to be traveling straight ahead, and less likely to be negotiating curves or changing lanes.
- Once a critical event had been initiated, older drivers were less likely to brake, steer, or otherwise maneuver their vehicles to avoid the crashes. *Note:* In the absence of objective signs such as tire skid marks, this information was typically unreported.

Table 6. 2002-2006 FARS descriptive results – crash characteristics

Crash Characteristics	Two-Vehicle Crashes (all drivers)				Single-Vehicle Crashes			
	60-69	70-79	80+	All ages	60-69	70-79	80+	All ages
First Harmful Event								
Non-collision	0.53	0.24	0.05	0.61	22.76	17.28	10.71	24.83
Coll non-fix obj.	0.21	0.12	0.10	0.20	4.28	5.55	5.99	3.09
Coll mv in transp	96.84	98.35	98.87	96.58	0.10	0.25	0.12	0.07
Coll mv not transp	0.17	0.06	0.15	0.16	2.60	3.02	4.20	2.05
Coll fixed object	2.24	1.23	0.83	2.44	70.19	73.89	78.81	69.90
Vehicle Role								
Striking	42.47	36.68	28.81	51.46	--	--	--	--
Struck	54.29	60.18	67.94	45.46	--	--	--	--
Manner of Collision								
Rear-end	5.90	5.98	5.22	6.40	--	--	--	--
Head-on	31.06	26.61	18.58	30.63	--	--	--	--
F→S, Right angle	36.45	42.75	51.54	35.58	--	--	--	--

Table 6. (Continued)

Crash Characteristics	Two-Vehicle Crashes (all drivers)				Single-Vehicle Crashes			
	60-69	70-79	80+	All ages	60-69	70-79	80+	All ages
F→S, Opp direct.	16.02	16.79	18.05	16.41	--	--	--	--
F→S, Other	3.65	3.54	3.94	3.70	--	--	--	--
Sideswipe	3.48	2.47	1.43	3.52	--	--	--	--
Initial Impact								
Front (12 hour)	59.36	46.06	33.47	62.35	50.61	57.76	63.79	42.09
Right side (1-5hrs)	14.80	19.47	24.91	15.25	12.88	11.30	11.92	15.30
Rear (6 hour)	3.81	3.31	2.31	3.37	0.43	0.72	0.46	0.87
Left side (7-11hrs)	21.58	30.92	38.97	18.35	12.52	11.67	9.97	15.24
Top/undercarriage	0.15	0.06	0.06	0.27	4.13	4.28	4.49	5.16
Non-collision	--	--	--	--	17.25	12.60	8.12	18.39
Vehicle Maneuver								
Going straight	72.32	61.91	51.97	73.06	71.94	75.15	73.29	65.98
Starting in lane	1.98	4.29	6.08	1.48	--	--	--	--
Stopped in lane	1.35	1.47	0.88	1.28	--	--	--	--
Passing	1.07	1.08	0.53	2.25	1.10	0.61	0.63	1.93
Right turn	0.55	0.77	1.23	0.44	0.28	0.22	0.41	0.35
Left turn	10.69	20.26	31.84	8.58	0.55	0.76	1.27	0.50
U-turn	0.81	1.47	1.58	0.57	--	--	--	--
Backing	0.07	0.12	0.13	0.08	0.25	0.40	0.58	0.12
Changing lanes	1.22	1.16	0.60	1.84	1.13	1.26	1.15	1.84
Negotiating curve	7.66	5.60	3.24	8.33	21.78	18.47	18.31	26.13
Avoiding Maneuver								
None	46.97	51.18	52.52	44.34	43.11	46.78	47.15	38.30
Braking	4.84	2.92	1.71	5.68	3.58	3.38	2.54	5.48
Steering	6.12	3.84	2.13	6.70	15.78	13.54	9.84	17.32
Braking + steering	3.59	2.12	0.78	4.10	4.25	3.53	2.99	5.11
(Not reported)	38.32	39.71	42.73	38.93	33.16	32.55	37.25	33.62

Driver-Related Crash Characteristics

Table 7 below summarizes results for up to four factors identified as contributing to each crash. Thus, a driver identified as both drowsy and making an improper lane change would appear twice in the table counts. In the case of two-vehicle crashes, the table reflects related factors for the at-fault driver. Also, it should be noted that the list of factors in this table represents only a partial listing, excluding those not specifically related to driving error (e.g., tire blowout, vision obscured by trees), and those cited very infrequently (such as driving under minimum speed, failure to take prescription medicine, and failure to signal).

Table 7. 2002-2006 FARS descriptive results – driver-related factors (partial list)

Driver Factors	Two-Vehicle Crashes At-fault Driver Only				Single-Vehicle Crashes			
	60-69	70-79	80+	All ages	60-69	70-79	80+	All ages
Drowsy, fell asleep	1.37	1.11	0.63	1.89	6.83	8.03	6.79	4.96
Ill, blackout	2.91	2.30	1.76	1.10	7.18	11.13	11.57	2.04
Medication/drugs	0.08	0.03	0.00	0.09	0.25	0.22	0.35	0.13
Alcohol/drugs/DUI	4.32	2.15	0.66	11.98	9.08	3.56	1.90	20.57
Inattentive	11.39	9.74	10.46	10.20	10.85	11.06	11.40	9.92
Other physical impairmt	0.36	0.40	0.47	0.18	0.80	1.48	1.55	0.30
Run off road	1.98	1.44	1.26	2.80	24.13	27.87	25.22	26.29
Improper tailing	1.05	1.26	1.04	1.37	0.23	0.32	0.17	0.13
Improper lane change	1.66	0.86	0.41	1.79	0.33	0.32	0.58	0.78
Failure to keep in lane	32.53	22.56	13.16	39.82	38.46	33.17	34.31	36.11
Improper entry/exit	0.44	0.68	0.79	0.29	0.03	0.07	0.35	0.05
Improper start/back	0.20	0.34	0.25	0.17	0.10	0.18	0.35	0.08
Prohibited pass	0.28	0.31	0.13	0.95	0.08	0.00	0.06	0.25
Passing insuf. distance	1.33	0.89	0.25	1.96	0.23	0.14	0.12	0.43
Erratic/reckless	4.08	3.20	2.51	7.25	7.58	5.69	6.91	10.75
Failure to yield	38.79	51.48	61.70	26.89	1.05	1.51	1.78	0.81
Failure to obey signal	18.26	17.27	18.79	17.30	2.23	3.24	5.01	2.12
Driving too fast	8.61	5.53	3.33	19.91	24.61	18.47	16.35	44.41
Wrong lane turn	0.12	0.22	0.19	0.11	0.00	0.00	0.00	0.01
Other improper turn	4.16	5.78	5.44	3.77	4.93	4.97	4.84	5.28
Wrong way	0.32	0.34	0.35	0.43	0.05	0.04	0.06	0.04
Wrong side of road	4.44	4.15	3.46	5.55	0.43	0.65	1.21	0.64
Stopping in road	0.32	0.43	0.19	0.31	0.03	0.07	0.06	0.02
Over-correcting	1.98	1.41	0.75	3.36	12.68	9.47	7.89	13.19
Weather	0.57	0.68	0.41	0.68	0.70	0.68	0.46	0.48
Glare	0.24	0.65	0.50	0.33	0.13	0.22	0.75	0.09
Cellular phone	1.21	0.83	0.72	1.27	1.10	0.76	0.35	1.28

With respect to two-vehicle crashes:

- Failure to yield was the most frequently cited related factor among older drivers. Overall, 27% of drivers failed to yield, but this percentage increased to 39% for drivers 60 to 69, 51% for drivers 70 to 79, and 62% for drivers 80 and older.
- As a group, older drivers were underrepresented in citations for failure to keep in proper lane (e.g., crossing the centerline, going straight in a turn lane), driving too fast, alcohol or drug use, and careless or reckless driving, all of which are important contributors to two-vehicle crashes overall.

With respect to single-vehicle crashes:

- Older drivers were somewhat more likely to be identified as ill or blacking out, drowsy or asleep, using medications or drugs (other than alcohol), and having some other physical impairment (missing limb, hearing loss, etc.). They were less likely to be identified as driving too fast, and somewhat less likely to have overcorrected. Otherwise, their related factor profile does not differ greatly from that of the general driving population.

Exposure-Adjusted Risk Factors for Fatal Two-Vehicle Crashes

This section provides results from the induced exposure analyses of the subset of two- vehicle fatal crashes in which one at-fault and one not-at-fault driver were identified. The not-atfault driver was assumed to be "an innocent victim," and as such, to represent the exposure level of his/her age group in the driving situation under study. Thus, the ratio of at-fault to not-at-fault drivers (crash involvement ratio, or CIR) represents the degree of over- (if greater than 1.0) or under- (if less than 1.0) involvement with respect to a given risk factor. Data tables supporting the following graphs are included in Appendix C.

Driver Factors

Figure 1 shows that older drivers' risk of involvement in fatal two-vehicle crashes remained "below average" for drivers 60 to 69, but rose sharply for older age groups. For drivers 70 to 79, the risk was nearly equivalent to that of teenage drivers, and for those 80 and older, it was four times higher than expected based on driving exposure. These results may reflect factors in addition to driving performance decrements, such as increased frailty and overall driving exposure characteristics.

The results in Figure 1 also present a "baseline" against which subsequent results in this section can be compared, i.e., unless a given factor produces an effect greater than 0.75 for drivers 60 to 69, 1.75 for drivers 70 to 79, and/or 4.00 for drivers 80 and older, it was not a strong risk factor for older driver involvement in a fatal two-vehicle crash. Conversely, if a factor produced an effect *lower* than the referenced values, it could be considered protective against crash involvement for a particular age group.

Figure 2 shows the same results separately for male and female drivers. The female CIR was somewhat higher at 60 to 69, and even more so at 70 to 79. The male CIR was slightly higher (4.1 to 3.9) among drivers 80 and older.

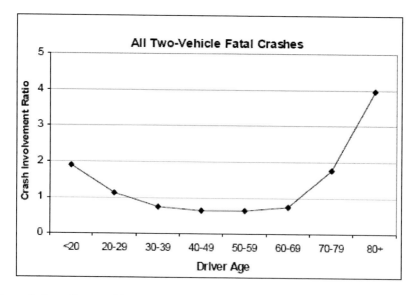

Figure 1. Overall two-vehicle fatal CIRs by driver age group

The effect of number of occupants in the vehicle is shown in Figure 3. Interestingly, an older driver was at greatest risk of crashing when one other occupant was in the vehicle, and at lowest risk when there were two or more other occupants. Although the presence of occupants can increase the likelihood of a crash being fatal (i.e., there are more opportunities for at least one of the occupants to be killed in the crash), without additional information such as passenger age this does not explain why having two or more passengers is "safer" than having just one other passenger. It is noteworthy that this effect increased with age.

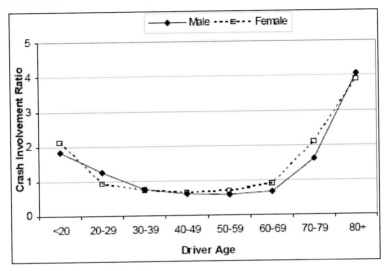

Figure 2. Fatal crash involvement ratios by driver gender

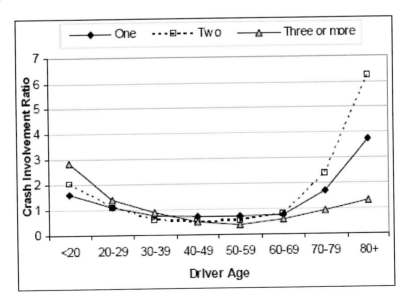

Figure 3. Two-vehicle fatal CIRs by total number of occupants in the vehicle

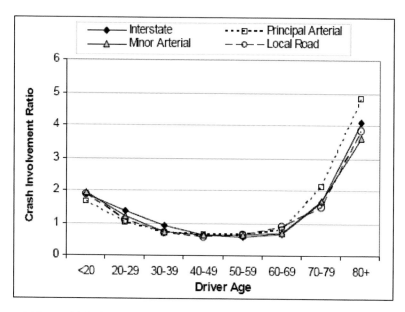

Figure 4. Two-vehicle fatal CIRs by roadway function class

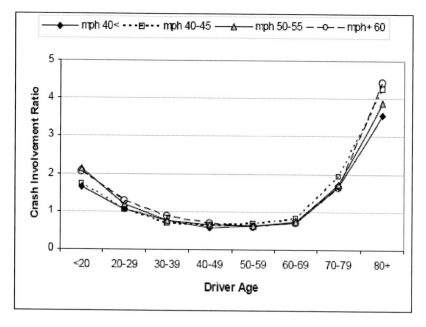

Figure 5. Two-vehicle fatal CIRs by roadway speed limit

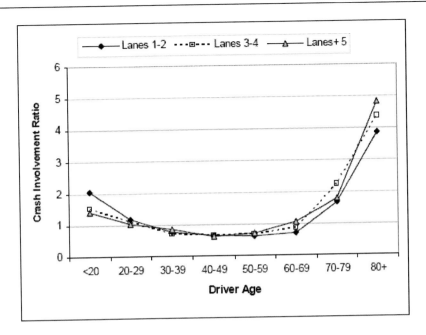

Figure 6. Two-vehicle fatal CIRs by number travel lanes

Roadway Factors

Figures 4-6 display results for roadway function class, posted speed limit, and number of travel lanes. For drivers 70 and older, the risk of involvement in fatal two-vehicle crashes was elevated when traveling on principal arterial roadways. The oldest drivers had a slight elevation in risk when traveling on higher speed roadways. Otherwise, 40 to 45-mph roadways presented the greatest risk to older drivers, a fact that likely reflects the increased presence of intersections and heavy traffic flow on these sorts of roadways. As might be expected, two-lane roadways were safer for older drivers than multilane roadways; and 5+ lane roadways posed added risk for drivers 80 and older.

More distinct differences emerge when examining specific roadway features and traffic control devices (Figures 7-9). As shown in Figure 7, older drivers, and especially those 70 and older, were at greatest risk of crashing at intersection and driveway locations, but were about as safe as younger drivers at non-junction locations. While these results were not especially surprising given the descriptive findings already reported, they demonstrate that the increased risk remained even when accounting for older drivers' (presumably) greater exposure to intersection locations.

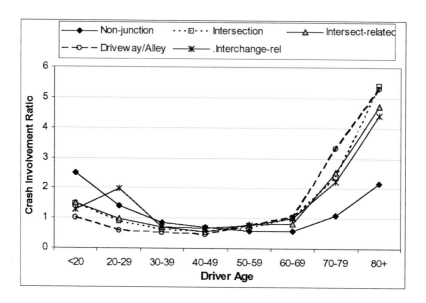

Figure 7. Two-vehicle fatal CIRs by roadway junction type

Figure 8 provides more detail about interchange locations, where drivers 70 and older demonstrated an elevated crash risk. Older drivers, especially those 70 and older, were most at risk when traveling through an intersection associated with an interchange, followed by negotiating an entrance or exit ramp. Risk levels at these locations were about equal to or greater than that of more standard intersection locations.

The greatest risk of a fatal two-vehicle crash occurred at non-signal-controlled intersections. In Figure 9, the overall CIR at intersections was repeated for comparison purposes in the blue diamond pattern. Compared to this overall CIR, the CIR for signal-controlled intersections was actually lower, especially for drivers 80 and older. Among 60 to 69 year-old drivers, the only situation posing increased risk was flashing signals. For 70 to 79 year-old drivers, flashing signals and stop and yield signs were associated with elevated risk (ratios of 2.9 for each, compared to 2.4 for all intersection locations). For drivers 80 and older yield sign locations were by far the most dangerous. Although not depicted in the figure due to scale limitations, the CIR at yield sign locations for drivers 80 and older was 26.0 this was based on 27 crash-involved drivers, *26 of whom were at fault*. Stop sign locations were also associated with a substantial increase in crash risk (CIR=7.5, compared to 5.4 overall).

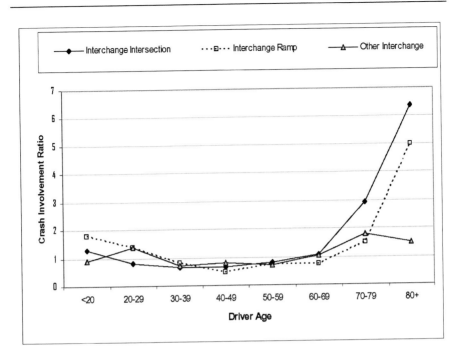

Figure 8. Two-vehicle fatal CIRs by interchange feature

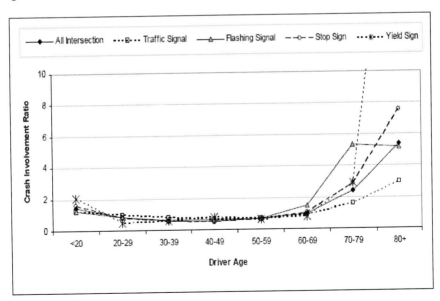

Figure 9. Two-vehicle fatal CIRs by intersection traffic control.

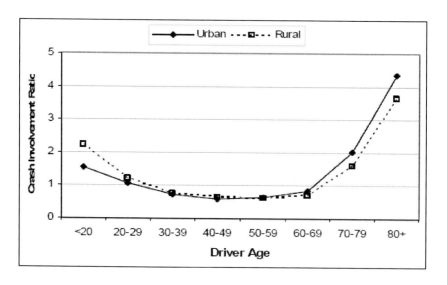

Figure 10. Two-vehicle fatal CIRs on urban versus rural roadways

Environmental Factors

Figure 10 presents results for fatal two-vehicle crashes occurring in urban versus rural locations (based on the FARS *Roadway Function Class* variable). In contrast to younger drivers, older drivers were at greater risk of involvement in a fatal two-vehicle collision when traveling on urban roadways. However, the increase in risk was relatively small, and likely reflected the increase in intersection crashes (and more dangerous side impacts) in urban areas.

The two figures that follow show risks of two-vehicle fatal crashes associated with driving under various light (Figure 11) and weather (Figure 12) conditions. In contrast to young drivers, who were overrepresented when driving at dawn, drivers 70 and over were at greatest risk when driving at dusk. Other lighting conditions did not appear to pose additional risk for older drivers, at least when compared to daytime driving.

In addition, older drivers were not at increased risk when driving in "bad" weather conditions such as rain, snow, or sleet. The absence of an increased at-fault crash risk in situations generally considered to be higher risk (such as nighttime driving or driving in adverse weather conditions) may reflect older drivers' tendency to self-regulate, and not drive under these conditions unless they feel capable.

Crash Factors / Vehicle Maneuvers

This section examines specific vehicle maneuvers identified in the descriptive results as problematic for older drivers. Results are based on the maneuver of the at-fault driver in the crash. For intersection locations, the maneuvers were examined with respect to the type of traffic control device.

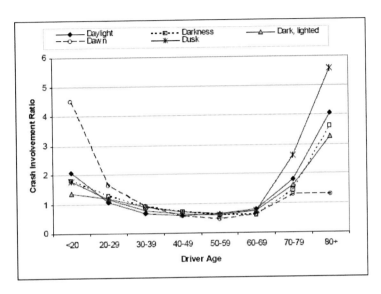

Figure 11. Two-vehicle fatal CIRs for various *light conditions*

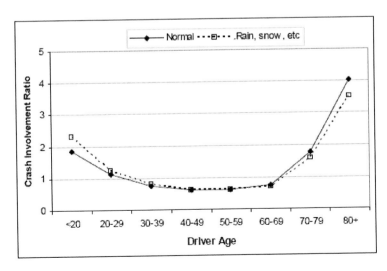

Figure 12. Two-vehicle fatal CIRs for normal and not normal *weather conditions*

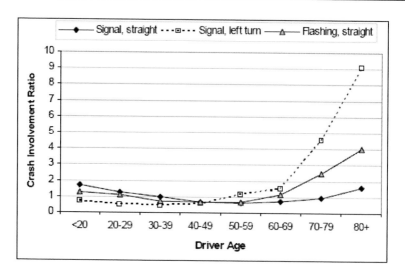

Figure 13. Two-vehicle fatal CIRs by *vehicle maneuver at signal controlled intersections*

Figure 13 summarizes available results for signal-controlled intersection crashes. Proceeding straight through a signal-controlled intersection posed minimal risk to older drivers, even those 80 and older. Risk was increased when the control was a flashing rather than a steady traffic signal. However, turning left posed the greatest risk to older drivers. Even at a signal-controlled intersection, they had a nine-fold increase in crash risk (compared to all drivers) after adjusting for exposure. Numbers for turning left at a flashing light were too small to analyze (only 55 fatal crashes across all age groups), but indicated substantial increased risk as well: of 11 drivers 70 to 79 involved in fatal two-vehicle crashes when turning left at flashing signals, *all* were at fault. For drivers 80 and older, all 7 drivers involved in this type of crash were at fault. Results with respect to right-turn maneuvers at signal-controlled intersections were too small to report.

Figure 14, a companion to Figure 13, presents results for various vehicle maneuvers at intersections controlled by a stop or yield sign, as well as driveways and alleyways (which function like yield signs when no control is present). Noting the change in scale for this graph (increasing from 1-10 to 1-20 CIRs), drivers 70 to 79 were most at risk when turning left at a stop-sign controlled intersection or when turning left out of a driveway. They are also at increased risk when first starting up at a stop sign (beginning to move forward without any notation of which way they were proceeding through the intersection). The results with respect to turning at a yield sign are not shown due to small numbers; but 11 of the 12 drivers 70 to 79 turning either left or right at a yield sign were at fault.

For drivers 80 and older, going straight at a yield sign emerged as the most dangerous maneuver. This might occur when merging onto a limited access roadway and having to check behind for traffic. Starting up or turning left at a stop sign increased risk 12 to 14-fold, while turning left out of a driveway or alley increased risk 8-fold. Results are not displayed for turning maneuvers at yield signs due to small cell counts; but all seven drivers 80 and older who were involved in such collisions were judged to be at fault.

Figure 15 shows results for various vehicle maneuvers at non-junction locations. They include situations where the at-fault driver was changing lanes or merging, passing, and starting in the lane. These older drivers were *not* at increased risk when passing, and only at slightly increased risk when changing lanes or merging. Results with respect to starting in the lane were less clear, in part because of smaller cell counts (17, 18, and 20 for 60 to 69, 70 to 79, and 80 and older, respectively), but also because it is not known what precipitated the starting maneuver.

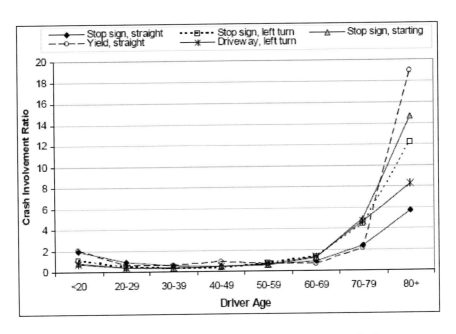

Figure 14. Two-vehicle fatal CIRs by *vehicle maneuver at sign controlled intersections and driveways*

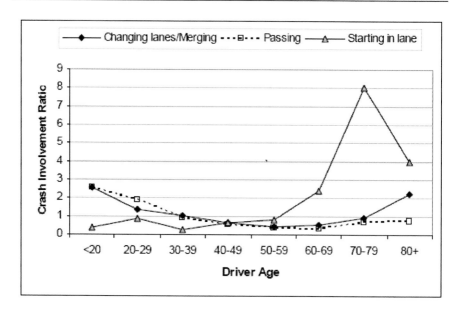

Figure 15. Two-vehicle fatal CIRs for at-fault *vehicle maneuvers at non-junction locations*

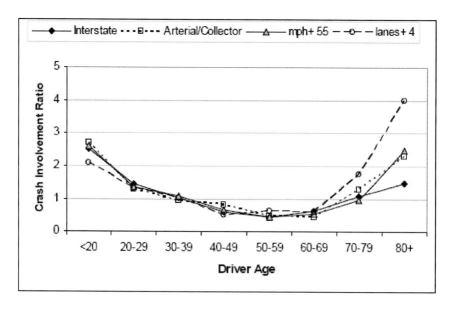

Figure 16. Two-vehicle fatal CIRs for *changing lanes or merging on various types of roadways*.

Results with respect to changing lanes or merging were further investigated for various road types in Figure 16. These results show some increase in risk for older drivers 70 and older on certain roadways, the risk does not exceed the average crash risk (4.0, see Figure 1) for this age group. Notwithstanding, changing lanes or merging was most risky for older drivers traveling on multilane roadways. It may be that older adults of all abilities encountered multilane roadways in their everyday driving, whereas only the more competent (and confident) choose to drive on Interstates or busier arterial and collector roadways. Of course, there is some degree of overlap among these various roadway classifications. It should be noted that results with respect to "4+ lane" are based on only 10 total drivers in the 80-and-older category (8 at- fault, 2 not-at-fault).

RESULTS OF GES DATA ANALYSIS

The NASS General Estimates System, or GES data, is a nationally representative probability sampling of all police-reported motor vehicle crashes in the United States. Approximately 56,000 police crash reports are identified and coded each year, then weighted to reflect an estimated six million total annual crashes. As previously described, the analysis files developed for the current study were restricted to eligible vehicle types (cars, utility vehicles, vans, and light trucks) and to single- and two-vehicle crashes (excluding pedestrian and bicycle crashes).

As with the earlier analyses of FARS data, this analysis was descriptive in nature and involved (1) crosstabulations of relevant driver, vehicle, roadway, environmental, and crash factor variables by driver age, for single- and two-vehicle crashes; and (2) more in-depth analysis of two-vehicle crash factors using the method of induced exposure. Cases with missing variable level values were excluded from the analyses rather than using available imputed values; according to the file documentation, variables containing imputed values are only recommended for use when generating single variable distributions.

Characteristics of Older Driver Crashes (All Severities)

Results in the following tables are based on the combined 2002-2006 weighted GES data and follow a similar format to that used in reporting the FARS results. Available variables are grouped according to driver, vehicle, roadway, environmental, and crash categories, although the specific variables and variable levels often differ. The percentages presented are column percents, and have been calculated with missing cases removed to facilitate comparisons between the single- and two-vehicle crash conditions, as well as with the FARS data.

Driver Characteristics

- Only a small percentage of drivers involved in two-vehicle police-reported crashes experienced fatal or incapacitating injuries. The percentages were higher for drivers in single-vehicle crashes, but still represented less than 5% of all crash-involved drivers. These percentages were slightly higher for drivers 60 to 69 and they increased with age.

Table 8. 2002-2006 GES descriptive results – driver characteristics

Driver Characteristics	Two-Vehicle Crashes				Single-Vehicle Crashes			
	60-69	70-79	80+	All ages	60-69	70-79	80+	All ages
Injury Severity								
Fatal (K)	0.08	0.22	0.39	0.07	0.83	1.38	1.25	0.53
Incapacitating (A)	1.46	1.86	2.15	1.31	4.32	3.42	5.34	4.26
Non-incap/evid. (B)	3.82	4.06	6.02	3.60	8.29	9.22	10.15	9.60
Possible (C)	11.00	9.85	9.51	10.45	8.49	10.26	11.90	10.28
None (O)	83.41	83.77	81.59	84.35	79.40	74.94	70.54	74.91
Gender								
Male	57.513	56.50	56.31	54.57	62.88	62.84	56.50	61.65
Female	42.49	43.50	43.69	45.43	37.12	37.16	43.50	38.35
Physical Impairment								
None	98.61	98.87	98.63	98.38	86.42	86.37	82.72	85.14
Occupants								
One	73.83	72.10	75.69	69.95	76.57	75.62	77.81	72.45
Two	20.46	23.43	22.37	19.94	18.02	21.01	20.20	18.45
Three+	5.71	4.47	1.94	10.10	5.41	3.36	1.98	9.11

- Males were overrepresented in both single- and two-vehicle crashes, although not to the extent shown in the FARS data. Similar to FARS, there was no clear trend with respect to age, except that females in the oldest age group were at increased risk of involvement in a single-vehicle collision.
- Older drivers were no more likely than the norm to have some physical impairment (loss of limb, loss of vision in one eye, hearing loss, etc.).
- As a group, older drivers were somewhat more likely to be the sole occupant in the vehicle, and much less likely as they aged to be driving with two or more other passengers. These findings are similar to those reported for the FARS data.

Vehicle Characteristics

- Consistent with the FARS data, with increasing age, older drivers who crashed were less likely to be driving utility vehicles and light trucks, and more likely to be driving standard automobiles or automobile derivatives.
- Also consistent with the FARS data, those 60 to 69 were more likely to drive newer model vehicles (less than 5 years old), while those 80 and older were more likely to be driving vehicles 10 years old or older.

Table 9. 2002-2006 GES descriptive results – vehicle characteristics

Vehicle Characteristics	Two-Vehicle Crashes				Single-Vehicle Crashes			
	60-69	70-79	80+	All ages	60-69	70-79	80+	All ages
Body Type								
Auto/auto deriv	58.85	69.95	80.19	59.76	53.63	64.00	80.26	58.74
Utility	11.88	7.30	4.25	14.82	11.64	6.70	3.32	14.24
Van	9.99	7.88	5.46	7.75	11.08	11.04	7.17	6.99
Light truck	19.27	14.88	10.11	17.67	23.66	18.26	9.25	20.03
Vehicle age								
Less than 5 years	41.67	37.95	31.85	38.03	40.83	39.59	31.69	36.43
5-9 years	32.20	32.52	32.94	34.06	31.88	31.10	31.55	34.41
10+ years	26.13	29.53	35.20	27.91	27.29	29.30	36.76	29.17

Roadway Characteristics

Table 10. 2002-2006 GES descriptive results – roadway characteristics

Roadway Characteristics	Two-Vehicle Crashes				Single-Vehicle Crashes			
	60-69	70-79	80+	All ages	60-69	70-79	80+	All ages
Interstate								
No	95.85	96.82	98.41	94.77	89.98	92.59	95.36	89.30
Yes	4.15	3.18	1.59	5.23	10.02	7.41	4.64	10.70
Speed Limit								
35 mph or less	48.49	50.18	54.26	48.02	31.87	40.50	55.91	33.91
40-45 mph	32.56	32.62	30.85	31.80	15.64	13.15	10.35	16.48
50-55 mph	13.73	12.90	12.21	13.64	34.38	31.49	22.86	32.40
60+ mph	5.20	4.30	2.68	6.53	18.11	14.86	10.88	17.21
Number of Travel Lanes								
1-2	46.95	46.89	47.57	47.81	85.16	85.87	84.79	83.33
3-4	33.96	33.91	31.72	34.25	11.31	11.25	11.75	13.29
5+	19.09	19.20	20.71	17.94	3.53	2.88	3.46	3.38
Relation to Junction								
Non-junction	22.71	19.34	15.36	25.96	82.99	78.58	73.94	81.58
Intersection	34.59	40.51	45.19	32.24	0.46	0.19	0.07	0.28
Intersection-related	21.93	18.91	16.97	22.56	7.29	8.25	14.34	9.32
Driveway/alley	14.38	15.44	18.61	12.82	4.73	8.11	7.49	3.45
Other non-interchng	2.83	2.80	1.84	2.70	2.45	2.94	2.63	1.91
Interchng-intersect	0.90	0.72	0.84	0.81	0.07	0.00	0.07	0.09
Interchange ramp	2.19	1.74	1.11	2.31	1.45	1.54	0.73	2.64
Interchange other	0.47	0.54	0.07	0.61	0.56	0.39	0.74	0.73
Traffic Control Device								
No device	47.10	45.27	44.94	49.70	91.62	91.51	86.94	92.15
Traffic signal	31.04	30.44	28.55	29.38	2.51	1.76	3.13	2.01
Flashing signal	1.09	1.03	1.00	1.14	0.10	0.15	0.05	0.13
Stop sign	16.68	19.53	22.26	15.86	1.83	2.39	5.33	2.38
Yield sign	2.40	2.42	1.71	2.47	0.08	0.04	0.24	0.21
Warning sign	0.91	0.60	0.73	0.82	3.08	2.67	3.11	2.42
Railroad marking	0.18	0.06	0.02	0.10	0.31	0.59	0.85	0.20

- The only roadway classification information available for the GES data was whether the crash did or did not occur on an Interstate highway. Consistent with the FARS data, older drivers' single- and two-vehicle crashes on Interstate highways decreased sharply with age.

- The same pattern of decreasing crash rates with increasing age was seen in the data for 60+ mph speed limits. In contrast, older adults were increasingly likely to be involved in crashes on roadways with speed limits of 35 mph or less. This was especially true for single-vehicle crashes, which increased from less than a third for drivers 60 to 69 to 56% for drivers 80 and older.

- Older drivers' single- and two-vehicle crash distributions with respect to number of travel lanes were similar to those for the overall driving population.

- As with the fatal crash data, older drivers were overrepresented in two-vehicle crashes at intersection and driveway/alley locations, and underrepresented in crashes at non-junction locations. They were also underrepresented in both single- and two-vehicle crashes occurring on interchange ramps.

- With respect to two-vehicle crashes, older drivers were no more likely than the overall driving population to crash at traffic signal locations, despite the overall increase in proportion of intersection crashes. They were, however, much more likely to crash at intersections controlled by stop signs. Relatively few older driver crashes occurred at yield sign locations, and they were not overrepresented compared to the overall crash-involved population.

- Although most older drivers' single-vehicle crashes occurred at non-junction locations, an increasing percentage with age were intersection-related, or occurred at driveway/alley locations (approximately 20% of the total for drivers 70+). Similar to the FARS data, there was an overrepresentation of single-vehicle crashes at railroad sign locations.

Environmental Characteristics

- Older drivers were substantially overrepresented in both single- and two-vehicle crashes occurring between the hours of 10 a.m. and 2 p.m., a finding likely related to their increased exposure during these hours. With increasing age, older drivers were less likely to crash in the evening hours, between 6 p.m. and 10 p.m.; however, even for the oldest age group a relatively high proportion (nearly 1 in 5) of single-vehicle crashes occurred between 6 p.m. and 10 p.m.

**Table 11. 2002-2006 GES descriptive results –
environmental characteristics**

Environmental Characteristics	Two-Vehicle Crashes				Single-Vehicle Crashes			
	60-69	70-79	80+	All ages	60-69	70-79	80+	All ages
Time of Day								
6:00am – 9:59am	15.88	14.48	13.27	16.41	18.90	15.37	15.06	17.00
10:00am – 1:59pm	31.64	37.89	39.45	24.44	19.73	26.95	30.95	13.84
2:00pm – 5:59pm	36.56	35.33	38.74	36.43	22.04	28.31	32.61	18.42
6:00pm – 9:59pm	12.89	10.49	7.22	16.31	24.87	21.39	17.53	21.63
10:00pm – 1:59am	2.36	1.27	1.15	4.70	9.11	4.54	2.23	16.68
2:00am – 5:59am	0.66	0.56	0.17	1.71	5.45	3.44	1.62	12.42
Light Condition								
Daylight	84.63	87.92	91.07	78.17	58.53	67.59	76.72	46.71
Dark	3.02	2.50	2.16	4.64	26.96	19.83	9.99	31.45
Dark, lighted	9.32	7.09	4.64	13.79	9.33	7.57	9.92	16.36
Dawn	0.96	0.59	0.30	0.95	2.60	1.93	1.30	3.21
Dusk	2.06	1.90	1.83	2.46	2.58	3.08	2.07	2.27
Weather conditions								
No adverse	87.72	87.96	89.40	85.95	83.65	86.57	85.10	78.85
Rain, fog, etc.	12.28	12.04	10.60	14.05	16.35	13.43	14.90	21.15

- The data revealed a strong pattern of increased single- and two-vehicle crashes during daylight hours, and decreased dark and dark but lighted crashes with increased driver age. Even drivers 60 to 69 were strongly overrepresented in daylight crashes; and for those 70 to 79, nearly 90% of two-vehicle crashes, and two-thirds of single-vehicle crashes, occurred during daylight hours.
- Older drivers were less likely than the overall driving population to crash during adverse weather, which likely reflects a decrease in driving exposure under these conditions.

Crash Characteristics

The crash experience of older persons summarized in Table 12 indicates that:

- The modest effect of drivers' increasing likelihood of being the struck, as opposed to the striking vehicle with increasing age was in sharp contrast to the data from fatal crashes. These results may be attributed at least in part to older drivers' increased fragility and likelihood of death, especially when struck in the side.

Table 12. 2002-2006 GES descriptive results – crash characteristics

Crash Characteristics	Two-Vehicle Crashes				Single-Vehicle Crashes			
	60-69	70-79	80+	All ages	60-69	70-79	80+	All ages
Vehicle Role								
Striking	45.83	50.07	54.26	50.88	--	--	--	--
Struck	52.72	48.63	44.05	47.63	--	--	--	--
Both	1.34	1.22	1.69	1.32	--	--	--	--
Initial Impact Point								
Front/corner	41.65	44.09	47.18	46.68	--	--	--	--
Right side	16.24	18.20	21.45	14.61	--	--	--	--
Back/corner	26.53	19.37	13.21	23.04	--	--	--	--
Left side	15.44	18.22	18.16	15.46	--	--	--	--
Top/under	0.02	0.05	0.00	0.04	--	--	--	--
Manner of Collision								
Rear-end	38.29	31.26	24.24	41.65	--	--	--	--
Head-on	3.16	2.91	3.13	3.34	--	--	--	--
Angle	49.57	56.58	64.32	45.29	--	--	--	--
Sideswipe/same directn	6.87	7.60	6.83	7.33	--	--	--	--
Sideswipe/opp directn	1.29	0.91	1.01	1.43	--	--	--	--
First Harmful Event								
Motor vehicle in trnsp.	99.03	99.21	99.35	98.81	--	--	--	--
Non-collision/rollover	--	--	--	--	11.70	7.41	7.30	13.59
Fixed object	--	--	--	--	41.33	44.26	53.04	52.40
Non-fixed object	--	--	--	--	31.50	27.37	13.50	21.58
Parked vehicle	--	--	--	--	15.48	20.96	26.16	12.42
Movement: Crit. Event								
Going straight	45.77	44.39	41.89	49.09	71.84	68.70	64.30	67.56
Decelerating in lane	7.64	5.71	4.31	7.20	0.73	0.69	1.42	0.90
Accelerating in lane	0.13	0.06	0.06	0.16	0.15	0.57	1.42	0.18
Starting in lane	3.49	4.08	4.87	3.38	0.29	0.24	0.03	0.15
Stopped in lane	15.25	10.97	6.37	14.11	0.08	0.01	0.02	0.06
Passing/overtaking	1.05	1.05	1.27	1.19	0.69	0.50	0.79	0.70
Leaving/entering park	0.83	0.60	0.59	0.62	1.98	3.34	4.08	1.12
Turning right	3.63	4.86	6.49	3.39	2.00	2.81	3.04	2.45
Turning left	14.52	19.94	25.93	12.93	1.86	2.44	4.37	2.93
U-turn	0.61	0.92	0.92	0.60	0.21	0.23	0.92	0.24
Backing (not parking)	1.85	1.42	1.62	1.36	5.98	7.10	7.85	3.42

Table 12. (Continued)

Crash Characteristics	Two-Vehicle Crashes				Single-Vehicle Crashes			
	60-69	70-79	80+	All ages	60-69	70-79	80+	All ages
U-turn	0.61	0.92	0.92	0.60	0.21	0.23	0.92	0.24
Backing (not parking)	1.85	1.42	1.62	1.36	5.98	7.10	7.85	3.42
Negotiating curve	1.51	1.21	0.95	2.02	11.80	11.22	10.15	17.63
Changing lanes	2.94	3.84	3.96	3.14	0.93	0.62	0.68	1.10
Merging	0.36	0.54	0.29	0.39	0.28	0.24	0.38	0.45

- Older drivers' two-vehicle crashes were also more likely to involve left or right side impacts, and less likely to involve a rear impact. The percentage of frontal impacts, however, remained high, at nearly half of all initial impacts.
- As with the FARS data, there was a strong pattern of increased involvement in angle collisions with driver age.
- Older driver single-vehicle crashes were more likely to involve an initial collision with a parked vehicle or, for those 60 to 69, another non-fixed object, and they were less likely to involve a non-collision rollover. They were also less likely to involve striking a fixed object, although these types of crashes still characterized nearly half of older drivers' single-vehicle collisions.
- Although not quite as high as with fatal crashes, older drivers were strongly overrepresented in two-vehicle collisions involving a left turn. They were also overrepresented in collisions involving right turns and, to a lesser extent, changing lanes. One out of every five drivers 70 to 79 and one out of four of the 80 and older age group were turning left at the time of their crashes.

Driver Contributing Factors

Noting the caveats in the footnotes, the results in Table 13 above reveal that:

- Older drivers were more likely to be identified as "inattentive/lost in thought" or "looked but didn't see" at the time of their crash. These two categories of driver distraction applied to 10 to 15% of older drivers in two-vehicle crashes for whom information was available.
- Older drivers were less likely to be cited for use of alcohol/drugs, speeding, reckless driving, or driving with a suspended or revoked license. However, they were much more likely to be cited for failure to yield when at-fault in a two-vehicle collision. Roughly a third of at-

fault drivers 60 to 69 were cited for failure to yield in their crash, increasing to 46% for drivers 80 and older.

Table 13. 2002-2006 GES descriptive results – driver contributing factors

Driver Characteristics	Two-Vehicle Crashes				Single-Vehicle Crashes			
	60-69	70-79	80+	All ages	60-69	70-79	80+	All ages
Driver Distraction[1]								
Not distracted	50.18	46.01	45.18	48.34	46.80	47.02	39.40	46.84
Looked but didn't see	3.57	4.94	6.47	3.06	1.05	1.28	1.25	0.81
Sleepy or fell asleep	0.19	0.11	0.14	0.22	4.02	4.97	5.91	4.21
Inattn., lost in thought	6.47	7.36	9.57	6.45	4.54	7.09	9.88	4.37
Violations Charged[2]								
Alcohol/drugs	3.37	1.01	0.12	4.92	2.12	0.84	0.60	8.65
Speeding	5.74	4.33	4.50	8.31	3.66	4.21	0.64	6.86
Reckless driving	1.08	1.01	0.61	1.75	0.51	0.42	0.25	2.64
Suspended/revoked lic	0.86	0.60	0.49	2.70	0.06	0.28	0.19	1.97
Failure to yield	34.17	42.31	46.02	26.61	0.06	0.00	0.06	0.06
Run light/stop sign	12.56	11.95	12.04	10.14	0.13	0.56	0.00	0.30
Violation, no details	3.30	3.36	2.74	4.04	0.84	0.84	0.16	1.71
Other violation[3]	45.96	40.22	39.33	55.28	13.09	11.31	12.92	20.22

[1] Based on all drivers in two-vehicle crashes. Information was not coded or not available from police crash reports for 35% of single-vehicle and 36% of two-vehicle crash drivers (in addition to ~6% missing). The only variable levels presented are those representing more than 1% of the total coded.

[2] Based on the at-fault driver only in the smaller sample of two-vehicle crashes where one driver was identified as at-fault and the second driver not-at-fault. Computed by combining up to four violations cited for each driver, so that the combined column percentages can total more than 100%.

[3] No further details provided.

Exposure-Adjusted Risk Factors for Two-Vehicle Police-Reported Crashes

As with the FRS data, the smaller database of two-vehicle crashes, in which one driver was identified at-fault and one not-at-fault, was used to identify situations in which older drivers were at increased risk of crashing, adjusted for their driving exposure. Specifically, tables of at- fault driver age crosstabulated by not-at-fault driver age were generated for selected variable levels and variable level combinations of interest, and the ratio of at-fault to not-at-fault drivers was computed within age categories. The graphs that follow plot these CIRs. Although the results are based on the weighted GES file, unweighted tables were also generated, and where the raw numbers were found to be small (generally involving cell counts less than 20), notation has been made in the text. The tables used to generate the graphs (based on the weighted GES data) are contained in Appendix D.

Driver Factors

Figure 17 shows changes in the CIR with driver age, both overall and separately for males and females. When comparing these results with those based on the fatal crash data in Figures 1 and 2, the most striking difference is in the shape of the curve. Rather than being "J- shaped," the curve generated by the GES data is decidedly "U-shaped," with older drivers showing increased risk that closely parallel those of younger drivers. Also, the increase in risk is not nearly as great: instead of peaking at 4.0 for drivers 80 and older involved in fatal crashes, the CIR for overall crash involvement was only 1.9 (identical to that of drivers under 20 years old). CIRs for males and females deviate only slightly from this overall trend.

These results suggest that at least some of the increase in crash risk seen in the FARS data is due to older adults' increased risk of dying in a crash, rather than any inherent increase in risk of being involved in a crash. If this is the case, then the degree of discrepancy may vary with the crash situation being examined (e.g., side impact crashes may be more likely to be affected by older drivers' greater fragility than rear-end crashes).

The following discussion will focus on situations where older drivers' risk of crashing was elevated, based on their "baseline" levels in Figure 17 of 0.73 for drivers 60 to 69 (well below "average" risk), 1.14 for drivers 70 to 79 (somewhat higher than average risk), and 1.91 for drivers 80 and older (nearly double the risk).

Figure 18 shows the effect of number of occupants in the vehicle on a driver's likelihood of involvement in a crash. These results are similar to those in Figure 3 for fatal crashes, and suggest a protective effect of having more than one other passenger in the vehicle. Having just one passenger was associated with an increased risk of crashing for the oldest drivers.

Results with respect to driver injury level are shown in Figure 19. Here, fatal (K) level injuries have been omitted due to small sample sizes in the raw data (31 fatalities). However, the results clearly show that drivers 70 and older were at increased risk of moderate and serious injuries. These trend lines closely mimic the "J-shaped" curve found in Figure 1 based only on fatal crash data.

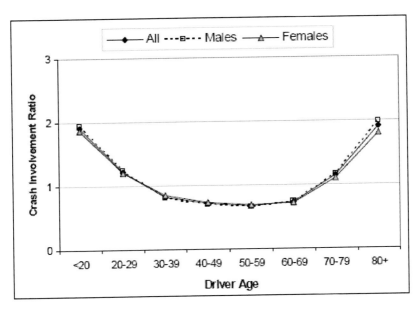

Figure 17. Two-vehicle CIRs for police-reported crashes, *overall* and by *driver sex*

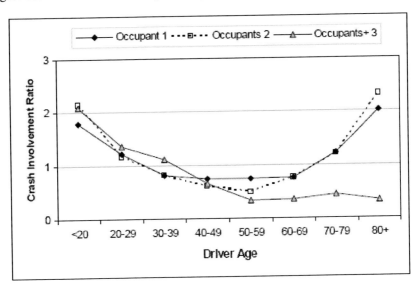

Figure 18. Two-vehicle CIRs for police-reported crashes by *number of occupants* in the vehicle

Roadway Factors

This section summarizes results related to roadway characteristics. In the GES data, the only variable describing roadway type indicates whether the crash occurred on an Interstate roadway. Results for this variable were based on relatively small raw sample sizes for drivers 80 and older. There were 36 drivers 80 and older involved in two-vehicle crashes on Interstate roadways (22 at-fault and 14 not-at-fault). The weighted crash involvement ratio for these drivers was 3.34, unexpectedly high, and much higher than that for other observed CIRs. The CIR for drivers 70 to 79 remained below 1.0.

The results for roadway speed limit in Figure 20 below show that for drivers 80 and older the CIR rose steadily with increased speed limits, peaking at 2.6 on 60+ mph roadways. Meanwhile, there was a conflicting finding for drivers 60 to 69 and 70-79, whereby <40 and 40- 45 mph roadways had higher CIRs than 60+ mph roadways. These results were similar to those based on FARS data (see Figure 5), and may be related to the types of crashes that occur on these roadways, and the greater likelihood of an older driver being at fault if the crash involved a turning maneuver.

Results with respect to number of travel lanes (Figure 21) show an increase in risk for drivers 80 and older traveling on 5+ lane roadways. Otherwise, the results mimic the FARS data results (see Figure 6), with only a slight increase in crash risk associated with multilane roadways beginning at age 70.

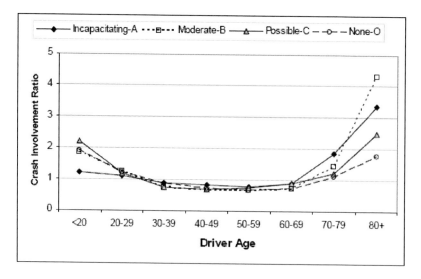

Figure 19. Two-vehicle CIRs for police-reported crashes by *driver injury severity*

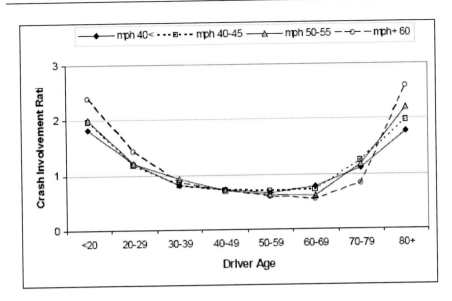

Figure 20. Two-vehicle CIRs for police-reported crashes by *roadway speed limit*

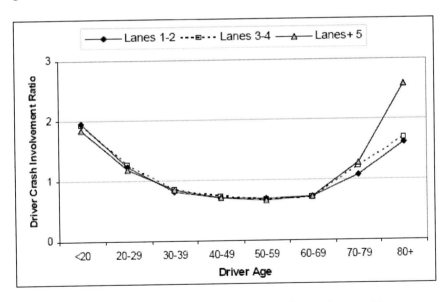

Figure 21. Two-vehicle CIRs for police-reported crashes by *number travel lanes*

Figure 22 combines results for speed limit and number of travel lanes. Not shown is the data point for drivers 80 and older, traveling on 5+ lane roadways with speed limits of 50 mph or greater. This data point, 6.34, was based on a raw sample CIR of 31/10, so is somewhat questionable. A second questionable data point in Figure 22 is that for drivers 80 and older traveling on 50-55 mph, 3-4 lane roadways. This data point (0.92) was lower than that for drivers 70 to 79, and was based on a raw sample CIR of 46/23. Anomalies notwithstanding, the two situations that appear to have posed the greatest risks to drivers 70 and older were highspeed 2-lane roadways, and multilane roadways with speed limits of 40-45 mph.

Figure 23, keyed to various roadway junction situations, shows older drivers were under-represented in crashes occurring at non-junction locations and those categorized as intersection- related. The latter might include, for example, rear-end collisions caused by traffic backed up at an intersection, or a driver making a late lane-change maneuver when approaching an intersection. The category of "other non-interchange," which appeared most prominently for drivers 80 and older, refers to crashes that occurred at same-grade lane channels; for example, when there was a left or right turn lane that was not a through lane (often marked by a traffic island). Otherwise, and consistent with the FARS data, intersections and interchanges posed the greatest risk to drivers 70 and above.

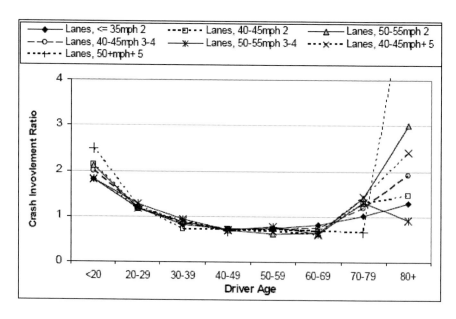

Figure 22. Two-vehicle CIRs for police-reported crashes by *number travel lanes* combined with *speed limit*

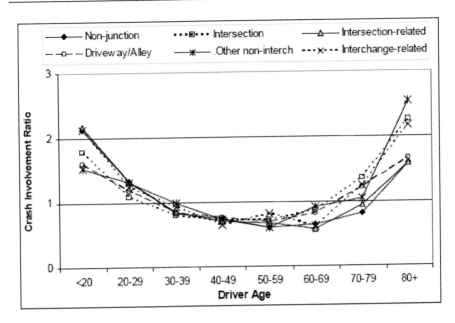

Figure 23. Two-vehicle CIRs for police-reported crashes by roadway junction

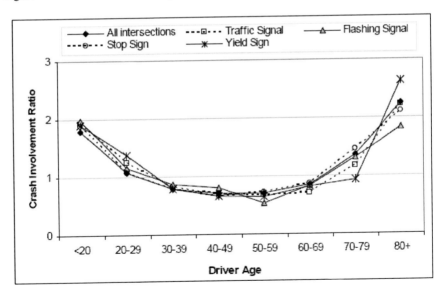

Figure 24. Two-vehicle CIRs for police-reported crashes by *traffic control device*

Findings with respect to traffic control device (Figure 24) show an elevated risk at yield sign locations for drivers 80 and older, but not for those

70 to 79. Stop sign and flashing signal controls were associated with higher risk of crashing for drivers in all age groups, but especially those 70 and older. These results, along with the finding that the risk of crashing at a signal-controlled intersection was slightly lower than the overall risk of crashing at an intersection are consistent with the FARS results.

Environmental Factors

Analyses included two environmental-related factors: light conditions and weather conditions at the time of the crash. Results with respect to light conditions (Figure 25) show similarities as well as differences as compared to the fatal crash data in Figure 11. Some of the differences can likely be attributed to low numbers in both datasets, especially for the "dawn" light condition. In the GES data, there were 30 raw cases of drivers 70 to 79, and only 10 for drivers 80 and older (which is why this data point is missing in Figure 25). But the larger categories of dark, and dark-lighted, also show some differences. Although both the FARS and GES data showed only a small increase in risk associated with such nighttime driving for drivers 70 to 79, the GES data showed increases in risk for drivers 80 and older in unlighted darkness. In contrast, the FARS data revealed no such increase in nighttime driving risk. It may be the case that, while nighttime driving was riskier for older drivers, the absence of higher speed nighttime driving reduced their risk of fatal crashes.

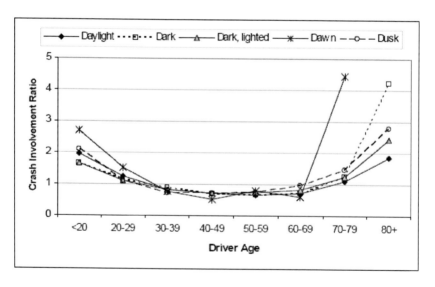

Figure 25. Two-vehicle CIRs for police-reported crashes by *light conditions*

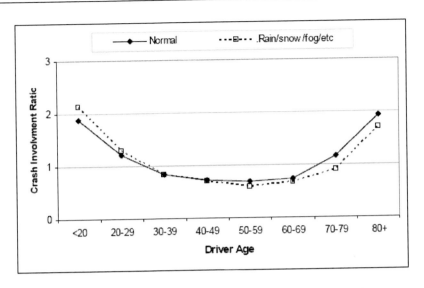

Figure 26. Two-vehicle CIRs for police-reported crashes by *weather conditions*

The impact of weather conditions (Figure 26) generally mirrored those found in the FARS data (Figure 12), and indicate no increased risk of being at-fault in a crash in unfavorable weather conditions. While this is somewhat counterintuitive, it may reflect older drivers' tendency to self-regulate and drive only when they feel comfortable doing so.

Crash-Related Factors

Crash-related factors examined in this final section include crash configuration or manner of collision; the at-fault vehicle's movement immediately prior to the critical crash event; and the initial point of impact for the at-fault vehicle.

The results in Figure 27 show older drivers to be underrepresented in rear-end collisions, and overrepresented in angle and sideswipe/same direction collisions, compared to other types of crashes. The angle collisions likely reflect their greater involvement in intersection crashes, especially when turning left. Sideswipe same-direction collisions are more difficult to characterize, but may relate to an increased difficulty changing lanes or staying in the proper lane.

Figure 28 presents information on at-fault vehicle maneuvers. There was a clear increase in crash risk when turning left or starting up in a travel lane. Risk also increased with age when turning right or changing lanes. The only maneuver that does not show a substantial increase relative to going straight ahead is passing/overtaking. As discussed earlier with respect to fatal crashes, this may be because older drivers tend to self-regulate and not pass or overtake other vehicles unless they are confident they can do so in safety.

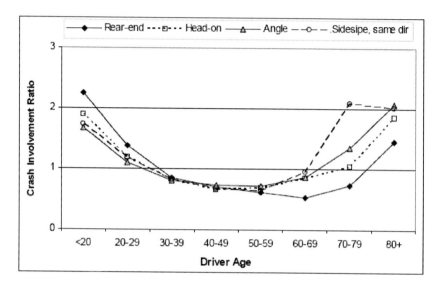

Figure 27. Two-vehicle CIRs for police-reported crashes by *manner of collision*

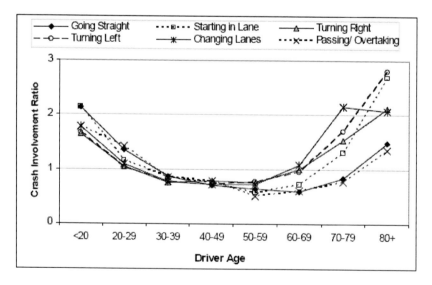

Figure 28. Two-vehicle CIRs for police-reported crashes by at-fault *vehicle movement* prior to critical event

Results for merging maneuvers are not shown due to small sample sizes in the raw data – only 8 drivers 80 and older and 14 70 to 79. Backing maneuvers and decelerating in travel lane crashes were also omitted from Figure 28, as neither was considerably elevated for older drivers (see Appendix D tables).

Figure 29 shows results for going straight and turning left maneuvers at signal-controlled and stop sign-controlled intersections. Clearly, the most dangerous situation for older drivers was turning left at a signal-controlled intersection, while the least dangerous was going straight at a signal-controlled intersection. Turning left or going straight at a stop sign posed about equal levels of risk, although going straight was slightly more challenging for drivers 80 and older. These results are similar to those presented in Figure 14 for fatal crashes, except that going straight at a stop sign location was found to be less dangerous relative to the other situations examined.

Other combinations of vehicle maneuver and traffic control device were also examined, but results were generally unstable at higher age levels due to small sample sizes in the raw GES data. For example, there were only 10 total incidents of drivers 80 and older turning left at yield sign locations, and 12 total incidents of drivers 80 and older going straight at yield signs.

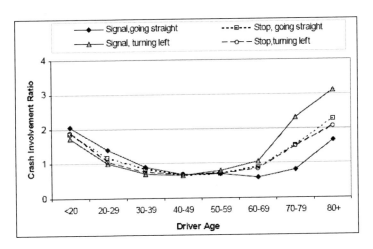

Figure 29. Two-vehicle CIRs for police-reported crashes by at-fault vehicle movement and traffic control device

Finally, Figure 30, based on data from the initial point of impact for the at-fault vehicle, shows older drivers were at increased risk of being struck in the side. Drivers 80 and older were especially vulnerable to right side impacts. This situation can occur when turning left at a stop sign and being struck by a vehicle approaching from the right – the classic "looked but didn't see" situation.

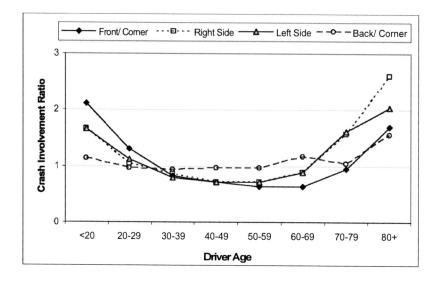

Figure 30. Two-vehicle CIRs for police-reported crashes by *initial impact point*

DISCUSSION

The FARS and GES analyses described in this report reveal the contemporary crash experience of older drivers on streets and highways in the United States. The over- and under- involvement of drivers 60 to 69, 70 to 79, and 80 and older in various crash types, reflecting specific maneuvers, traffic situations, and roadway/environmental conditions, has been highlighted through tabular summaries and accompanying discussion. For subsets of the two- vehicle crash data within each national database, crash involvement ratios based on the comparison of at-fault to not-at-fault drivers within groups of drivers younger than 20 to 80 and older, have provided additional, exposure-adjusted estimates of the magnitude of particular risk factors.

Inspection of these findings often reveals a somewhat attenuated U-shaped curve relating crash experience to driver age; this is to be expected when young, novice driver data are collapsed into a single category of under-20s, and when analyses specifically focus on two- vehicle crashes (omitting single-vehicle run-off-road crashes where teens are strongly overrepresented).

However, the express purpose of these analyses was to tease out differences among older driver cohorts. In that vein, it is useful to reiterate several broad trends observed in these data.

First, across this entire set of analyses there is little evidence of elevated risk for drivers 60 to 69, the "young-old." Most often, the data only begin to demonstrate a substantial upturn in crash experience for drivers 70 to 79, with over-representation for many crash types then accelerating more sharply for drivers 80 and older. This understanding can help target materials to educate older drivers about particular risk factors to the appropriate age cohorts, and suggests that engagement in health/wellness programs by seniors who are even well into their seventies may be a potent strategy to extend the safe driving years.

Another notable pattern in these data were crash involvement ratios for older age groups that did *not* bear out conventional wisdom about certain situations being especially risky for these drivers, such as merging, changing lanes, driving on Interstate highways, and driving in bad weather. The avoidance of bad weather (and nighttime) driving may be attributed to self-regulation, i.e., older people choosing not to drive in situations where they do not feel comfortable; thus, only the most skillful or confident older drivers may have been represented in the data. For non-discretionary travel, selecting routes that minimize or eliminate requirements for certain high-demand maneuvers may be an effective behavioral countermeasure for older drivers.

In comparing the crash involvement ratios calculated from the two national databases, those generated from FARS data were consistently higher than those generated from GES data. This may be interpreted as evidence of an added contribution of frailty—especially in angle crashes—on top of any risk due to age-related changes in the functional abilities needed to drive safely.

Finally, the handful of situations that appeared most problematic for older drivers reinforce and extend relationships by now well established in the technical literature. Left- turning movements are highlighted in this regard, as are movements at stop-sign-controlled intersections. High-speed 2-lane roadways and multi-lane roads with speed limits of 40 to 45 mi/h (e.g., suburban arterials) were associated with heightened older driver crash involvement. For fatal crashes, both "young-old" and "old-old" drivers were more likely to make errors at intersections controlled by flashing signals; and an error negotiating a yield-sign-controlled intersection was the reason for the crashes in 26 of 27 such incidents for drivers 80 and older.

Situations that have proven risky for older drivers often include complex visual searches, and information from multiple sources that must be processed rapidly under divided attention conditions. These are conditions where context-appropriate driver behavior often depends less upon conformity to formal or informal rules than to judgment or "executive function." This converges substantially with the cluster of cognitive abilities validated as significant predictors of at-fault crashes by older drivers in previous NHTSA research (see Staplin, Gish, and Wagner, 2003). Conceivably, the results of these national crash data analyses will help guide the development of materials and programs that both inform individuals as they seek to self-regulate their exposure to risky situations, and support health care givers as they counsel their older patients about steps they can take to keep driving safely longer.

APPENDIX A: VARIABLE LEVELS FOR FARS-RELATED FACTORS – DRIVER LEVEL VARIABLE USED IN DETERMINING FAULT

Manslaughter/homicide	Yield sign	Wheelchair	Oper Inexperience
Willful reckless	Traffic control dev	Road Rage	Unfamiliar w/ Road
Unsafe reckless	Turn violation not RTOR	Previous Injury	Stopping in Road
Inattentive	Improper turn/method	Other Physical	Underride Truck
Fleeing/eluding police	Fail to signal	Mentally Challenged	Over Correcting
Fail to obey police	Yield to emergency veh	Prohibited Trafficway	
Hit-and-run	Fail to yield	Improper Tailing	
Serious violation	Entering intersection	Improper Lane Change	
Intoxicated	Turn/yield/sig viol	Not in Lane	
Driving impaired	Wrong way/one way rd	Driving Shoulder	
Under Influence	Dr wrong side of rd	Improper Entry/Exit	
Drinking & operating	Unsafe passing	Improper Start/Back	
Detectable alcohol	Pass on right off road	Open Vehicle Closure	
Refused test	Pass stopped school bus	Prohibited Pass	
Alc/drug impairment	Fail to give way	Pass Wrong Side	
Racing	Follow too closely	Pass Insufficient Distance	
Speeding	Passing/following vehicle	Erratic/Reckless	
Unreasonable speed	Unsafe/illegal lane change	Failure to Yield	

Exceed spec speed limit	Improper use of lane	Failure to Obey	
Flashing red	Drowsy, asleep	Under Minimum Speed	
Energy speed	Spec vehicle lane rules	Around Barrier	
Driving too slow	Motorcycle lane viols	Fail to Observe Warn	
Speed related viols	Motorcyc hitched oth veh	Fail to Signal	
Red signal	Any lane violations	Driving too Fast	
Improper turn on red	Ill, blackout	Racing	
Flashing signal	Emotional	Wrong Lane Turn	
Disobey signal	Drugs-medication	Other Improper Turn	
Violate RR X-ing	Other drugs	Wrong Way	
Stop sign	Inattentive	Wrong Side of Road	

APPENDIX B: FAULT DEFINITION RULES IN FARS AND GES ANALYSES

The FARS fault definitions are as follows:

contributing factor values: 1-9,11,13,18,26,27,28-36,38-42,44-48, 50-55,58 or violation values 1-7,9, 11-14,16, 18, 19, 21-26,29, 31-39, 41-43,45,46,48,49,51-56, 58,59,61-63,66,67,69 earned the designation "at fault."

We paid attention to how many vehicles were at fault according to the following rules:
update fault2 set type='Single, At Fault' where ve_forms=1 and fault=1;
update fault2 set type='Single, Not At Fault' where ve_forms=1 and fault=0;
update fault2 set type='Two, At Fault' where ve_forms=2 and fault=1 and accfaults=1;
update fault2 set type='Two, Not At Fault' where ve_forms=2 and fault=0 and accfaults=1;
update fault2 set type='Two, Both At Fault' where ve_forms=2 and fault=1 and accfaults=2;
update fault2 set type='Two, None At Fault' where ve_forms=2 and fault=0 and accfaults=0;

update fault2 set type='Multi, At Fault' where ve_forms>2 and fault=1 and accfaults=1;

update fault2 set type='Multi, Not At Fault' where ve_forms>2 and fault=0 and accfaults=1;

update fault2 set type='Multi, None At Fault' where ve_forms>2 and fault=0 and accfaults=0;

update fault2 set type='Multi, Multi At Fault' where ve_forms>2 and accfaults>1;

GES fault definition only used viols:

Violations 1-4,6,7,97,98 ='at fault'

0,5='not at fault'

50='uncertain fault'

95,96,99='unknown'

APPENDIX C: 2002-2006 FARS DATA

Results Tables for At-Fault Crash Involvement Ratios for Two-Vehicle Crashes*

Driver Characteristics

Driver Age	All (N=37,090)	Gender		Driver Drinking (N=8,408)	Number Occupants		
		Male at Fault (N=24,683)	Female at Fault (N=12,280)		1 (N=22,617)	2 (N=9,334)	3+ (N=5,123)
<20	1.91	1.84	2.10	0.99	1.62	2.02	2.84
20-29	1.14	1.25	0.92	1.49	1.09	1.11	1.38
30-39	0.75	0.76	0.73	1.09	0.78	0.59	0.91
40-49	0.63	0.62	0.65	0.91	0.71	0.49	0.53
50-59	0.63	0.59	0.70	0.62	0.71	0.55	0.38
60-69	0.74	0.68	0.88	0.36	0.75	0.81	0.58
70-79	1.76	1.60	2.07	0.63	1.68	2.38	0.94
80+	3.98	4.05	3.89	0.68	3.75	6.24	1.33

Roadway Factors

Driver Age	Speed Limit				Number Traffic Lanes			
	<40 mph (N=5,556)	40-45 mph (8,599)	50-55 mph (N=15,788)	60+ mph (N=6,598)	1-2 Lanes (N=27,977)	3-4 Lanes (N=7,630)	5+ Lanes (N=1,108)	
<20	1.65	1.72	2.13	2.04	2.05	1.52	1.40	
20-29	1.06	1.05	1.18	1.27	1.17	1.07	1.03	
30-39	0.75	0.67	0.74	0.86	0.76	0.70	0.84	
40-49	0.57	0.62	0.64	0.67	0.63	0.63	0.62	
50-59	0.61	0.66	0.63	0.58	0.61	0.68	0.71	
60-69	0.78	0.80	0.72	0.70	0.71	0.84	1.04	
70-79	1.68	1.93	1.72	1.65	1.66	2.21	1.80	
80+	3.55	4.24	3.86	4.41	3.85	4.37	4.84	

Driver Age	Roadway Function Class (combined U/R)				Route Signing (Not in Figures)				
	Interstate (N=4,038)	Prin. Art. (N=11,021)	Minor Art. (N=8,730)	Local Rd (N=4,644)	Interstate (N=2,664)	US Hwy (N=7,827)	State Hwy (N=12,922)	County (N=6,124)	Local 5,908
<20	1.88	1.65	1.95	1.87	2.06	1.73	2.04	2.11	1.63
20-29	1.36	1.03	1.22	1.09	1.40	1.04	1.19	1.11	1.11
30-39	0.92	0.69	0.72	0.69	0.99	0.71	0.72	0.74	0.72
40-49	0.65	0.65	0.63	0.57	0.67	0.65	0.63	0.62	0.59
50-59	0.57	0.64	0.63	0.62	0.57	0.64	0.62	0.64	0.62
60-69	0.67	0.78	0.70	0.89	0.57	0.81	0.74	0.66	0.85
70-79	1.64	2.13	1.69	1.49	1.56	2.03	1.72	1.67	1.65
80+	4.10	4.83	3.61	3.83	3.67	4.84	4.10	3.62	3.39

* Entries placed in parentheses indicate small cell counts, generally 20 or fewer cases.

Driver Age	Interchange Related		Other (N=264)
	Intersection(N=461)	Ramp(N=176)	
<20	1.30	1.78	0.90
20-29	0.82	1.37	1.38
30-39	0.65	0.80	0.73
40-49	0.66	0.49	0.81
50-59	0.80	0.75	0.73
60-69	1.08	0.75	1.06
70-79	2.94	1.50	1.80
80+	6.38	(5.00)	(1.50)

Roadway Characteristics – Junction

Driver Age	Non-Junction (N=19,929)	Intersection (N=13,743)	Intersection-Related (N=1,124)	Driveway/ Alley (N=1,200)	Interchange-Related (N=905)
<20	2.50	1.47	1.49	1.02	1.27
20-29	1.40	0.87	0.98	0.58	1.07
30-39	0.86	0.61	0.71	0.52	0.70
40-49	0.69	0.55	0.55	0.47	0.67
50-59	0.58	0.68	0.78	0.77	0.75
60-69	0.57	0.99	0.83	1.05	1.00
70-79	1.09	2.39	2.53	3.33	2.23
80+	2.15	5.40	4.72	5.31	4.41

Traffic Control at Intersection Locations

Driver Age	Traffic Signal (N=3,747)	Flashing Signal (N=257)	Stop Sign (N=7,033)	Yield Sign (N=203)
<20	1.26	1.25	1.59	2.06
20-29	1.02	0.84	0.81	0.52
30-39	0.81	0.63	0.54	0.60
40-49	0.63	0.66	0.49	0.81
50-59	0.71	0.71	0.67	0.63
60-69	0.91	1.53	1.04	0.79
70-79	1.63	5.33	2.87	2.90
80+	2.98	5.20	7.53	26.0

Crash Characteristics

Changing Lanes and Merging

Driver Age	Change Lanes/Merge on Interstate (N=612)	Change Lanes/Merge On Arterial/ Collector(N=576)	Change Lanes/Merge Speed Limit 55+ (N=911)	Change Lanes/Merge 4+ Lanes (N=355)
<20	2.53	2.70	2.60	2.09
20-29	1.46	1.30	1.35	1.33
30-39	1.03	0.94	1.09	1.02
40-49	0.61	0.81	0.66	0.52
50-59	0.44	0.49	0.45	0.65
60-69	0.64	0.44	0.55	0.60
70-79	1.10	1.29	0.97	1.75
80+	(1.50)	2.29	2.50	(4.00)

Two-Vehicle Crash Configurations (Manner of Collision) at Intersections (not presented in Figures in this report)

Driver Age	Front to Rear (N=256)	Front to Front (N=894)	Front-to-Side Same Dir. (N=2726)	Front-to-Side Opp Dir (N=2,254)	Front-to-Side Right Angle (N=9,589)
<20	1.05	1.40	2.05	1.21	1.54
20-29	1.07	0.86	0.98	0.72	0.90
30-39	1.14	0.69	0.43	0.57	0.60
40-49	0.63	0.65	0.57	0.55	0.54
50-59	0.64	0.69	0.59	0.76	0.66
60-69	0.96	0.94	1.33	1.04	0.98
70-79	1.41	1.62	2.06	2.76	2.48
80+	1.72	4.89	8.50	5.49	5.83

Two-Vehicle Crash Configurations (Manner of Collision) at Non-Junction Locations (not presented in Figures in this report)

Driver Age	Front to Rear (N=1,656)	Front to Front (N=10,015)	Front-to-Side Same Dir. (N=484)	Front-to-Side Opp Dir (N=3,129)	Front-to-Side Right Angle (N=2,240)	Sideswipe Same Dir (N=573)	Sideswipe Opp Dir (N=548)
<20	1.79	2.07	1.81	4.05	2.82	2.21	3.15
20-29	1.77	1.41	1.27	1.47	1.17	1.24	1.37
30-39	1.03	0.90	0.76	0.75	0.68	0.95	0.94
40-49	0.74	0.78	0.67	0.56	0.53	0.64	0.77
50-59	0.47	0.64	0.63	0.46	0.51	0.64	0.64
60-69	0.52	0.56	0.79	0.54	0.76	0.62	0.52
70-79	0.86	0.97	1.69	1.19	2.21	1.41	0.82
80+	1.20	1.58	3.29	3.00	5.90	(3.00)	1.15

Vehicle Maneuver and Traffic Control Device for Intersection and Non-Junction Locations (Other movements – starting in lane, stopping in lane, turning right – insufficient *N*s)

Driver Age	Intersection w/ Signal		Intersection w/ Stop Sign			Intersection w/ Yield Sign
	Going Straight (N=2,491)	Turning Left (N=1,124)	Going Straight (N=4,769)	Turning Left (N=1,458)	Starting (N=578)	Going Straight (N=148)
<20	1.69	0.69	1.94	1.12	0.88	2.08
20-29	1.28	0.51	0.94	0.51	0.46	0.62
30-39	0.99	0.45	0.61	0.37	0.37	0.59
40-49	0.66	0.56	0.52	0.37	0.49	0.92
50-59	0.60	1.16	0.65	0.73	0.63	0.71
60-69	0.70	1.54	0.95	1.34	1.31	0.65
70-79	0.94	4.56	2.35	4.45	4.91	2.13
80+	1.59	9.08	5.69	12.21	14.60	19.00

Driver Age	Intersection w/ Flashing Light Going Straight(N=176)	Driveway/Alley Turning Left(N=647)	Non-Junction		
			Passing (N=1,337)	Changing Lanes (N=1,068)	Starting in Lane (N=92)
<20	1.29	0.78	2.54	2.56	(0.36)
20-29	1.12	0.46	1.89	1.39	0.86
30-39	0.74	0.41	0.93	1.03	0.28
40-49	0.67	0.50	0.54	0.66	0.63
50-5 9	0.68	0.68	0.40	0.46	(0.82)
60-69	1.17	1.36	0.35	0.55	(2.40)
70-79	(2.50)	4.69	0.73	0.93	(8.00)
80+	(4.00)	8.26	0.74	2.25	(4.00)

Environmental Factors

Driver Age	Light Condition			Weather Condition			
	Daylight (N=23,510)	Darkness (N=7,456)	Dark, Lighted (N=4,490)	Dawn (N=685)	Dusk (N=906)	Normal (N=31,726)	Rain, snow, etc. (N=5,140)
<20	2.08	1.81	1.37	4.50	1.77	1.86	2.31
20-29	1.05	1.28	1.18	1.64	1.16	1.12	1.25
30-39	0.67	0.88	0.88	0.91	0.77	0.73	0.80
40-49	0.59	0.71	0.71	0.58	0.63	0.63	0.63
50-59	0.64	0.59	0.63	0.45	0.60	0.63	0.62
60-69	0.78	0.60	0.73	0.61	0.73	0.75	0.69
70-79	1.80	1.44	1.60	1.29	2.62	1.78	1.59
80+	4.04	3.60	3.27	(1.29)	5.58	4.04	3.52

Driver Age	Crash Location Urban[b]	
	Rural (N=15,023)	(N=21,517)
<20	1.55	2.21
20-29	1.08	1.20
30-39	0.72	0.77
40-49	0.59	0.66
50-59	0.65	0.61
60-69	0.83	0.69
70-79	2.01	1.61
80+	4.36	3.66

* Based on Roadway Function Class variable

APPENDIX D: 2002-2006 GES DATA

Results Tables for at-Fault Crash Involvement Ratios for Two-Vehicle Crashes*

Driver Characteristics

Driver Age	All	Gender		Number Occupants		
		Male	Female	1	2	3+
<20	1.91	1.94	1.87	1.80	2.14	2.10
20-29	1.22	1.23	1.20	1.22	1.17	1.36
30-39	0.83	0.81	0.86	0.81	0.81	1.12
40-49	0.72	0.71	0.74	0.75	0.61	0.65
50-59	0.67	0.66	0.69	0.75	0.50	0.34
60-69	0.73	0.73	0.72	0.76	0.77	0.36
70-79	1.14	1.16	1.11	1.22	1.20	0.44
80+	1.91	1.99	1.81	2.02	2.33	0.34

Driver Injury Severity

Driver Age	Killed (K) *	Incapacit. (A)	Moderate (B)	Possible (C)	Non e (O)
<20	--	1.20	1.84	2.20	1.90
20-29	--	1.09	1.24	1.17	1.22
30-39	--	0.87	0.73	0.75	0.85
40-49	--	0.82	0.66	0.68	0.72
50-59	--	0.77	0.66	0.74	0.67
60-69	--	0.87	0.72	0.87	0.71
70-79	--	1.85	1.42	1.22	1.10
80+	--	3.34	4.30	2.48	1.75

* Omitted, since only 31 total fatalities in the raw data.

---

* Entries placed in parentheses indicate small cell counts in the raw data, generally 30 or fewer cases.

Crash Characteristics

Manner of Collision (Crash Configuration)

Driver Age	Rear-end	Head-on	Angle	Sideswipe, Same Dir.
<20	2.25	1.89	1.67	1.73
20-29	1.38	1.19	1.10	1.17
30-39	0.85	0.82	0.81	0.83
40-49	0.71	0.66	0.74	0.68
50-59	0.62	0.69	0.72	0.65
60-69	0.53	0.85	0.87	0.96
70-79	0.74	1.05	1.36	2.09
80+	1.46	1.85	2.07	2.02

At-fault Vehicle Movement Prior to Critical Event

Driver Age	Going Straight	Decel. in Lane	Starting in lane	Passing/ Overtaking	Turning Right	Turning Left	Backing Up	Changing Lanes	Merging
<20	2.14	1.96	2.13	1.78	1.64	1.67	1.44	1.78	1.52
20-29	1.35	1.28	1.15	1.42	1.04	1.03	1.03	1.09	1.55
30-39	0.86	0.89	0.85	0.85	0.75	0.76	0.83	0.76	0.82
40-49	0.70	0.85	0.75	0.79	0.78	0.71	0.90	0.72	0.62
50-59	0.63	0.68	0.57	0.51	0.75	0.76	1.09	0.72	0.44
60-69	0.58	0.41	0.71	0.60	0.99	0.95	1.24	1.08	1.71
70-79	0.83	1.01	1.31	0.77	1.53	1.70	0.90	2.15	2.47
80+	1.48	1.77	2.69	(1.35)	2.12	2.80	0.99	2.07	0.92

At-fault Vehicle Initial Impact Point

Driver Age	Front/ Corner	Right Side	Left Side	Back/ Corner
<20	2.12	1.66	1.66	1.13
20-29	1.31	1.04	1.12	0.96
30-39	0.83	0.85	0.80	0.94
40-49	0.71	0.72	0.71	0.96
50-59	0.64	0.72	0.72	0.97
60-69	0.64	0.89	0.89	1.17
70-79	0.95	1.57	1.62	1.04
80+	1.69	2.60	2.04	1.56

Roadway Characteristics

Driver Age	Interstate	
	Yes	No
<20	2.31	1.90
20-29	1.38	1.21
30-39	0.89	0.83
40-49	0.71	0.72
50-59	0.63	0.68
60-69	0.66	0.73
70-79	0.70	1.15
80+	3.34	1.89

Driver Age	Speed Limit				Number Traffic Lanes		
	<40 mph	40-45 mph	50-55 mph	60+ mph	1-2 Lanes	3-4 Lanes	5+ Lanes
<20	1.82	1.98	2.01	2.38	1.96	1.93	1.84
20-29	1.21	1.17	1.21	1.43	1.23	1.26	1.19
30-39	0.82	0.81	0.92	0.87	0.81	0.84	0.85
40-49	0.73	0.71	0.71	0.71	0.71	0.72	0.71
50-59	0.67	0.70	0.63	0.60	0.69	0.67	0.66
60-69	0.78	0.72	0.62	0.55	0.73	0.71	0.73
70-79	1.11	1.25	1.18	0.83	1.07	1.21	1.27
80+	1.77	1.98	2.21	2.59	1.62	1.70	2.58

Junction

Driver Age	Non-Junction	Intersection	Intersection-Related	Driveway/ Alley	Other Non-Interchange	Interchange-Related
<20	2.13	1.79	2.17	1.60	1.53	2.13
20-29	1.33	1.08	1.33	1.19	1.31	1.25
30-39	0.83	0.80	0.85	0.84	0.98	0.93
40-49	0.74	0.72	0.70	0.76	0.73	0.65
50-59	0.60	0.72	0.67	0.68	0.60	0.82
60-69	0.64	0.86	0.57	0.81	0.91	0.61
70-79	0.82	1.36	0.95	1.22	1.04	1.25
80+	1.58	2.26	1.59	1.66	(2.55)	(2.17)

Traffic Control

Driver Age	None	Traffic Signal	Flashing Signal	Stop Sign	Yield Sign
<20	1.94	1.94	1.99	1.89	1.90
20-29	1.24	1.26	1.16	1.08	1.38
30-39	0.84	0.83	0.87	0.79	0.80
40-49	0.75	0.70	0.81	0.67	0.67
50-59	0.65	0.69	0.54	0.73	0.65
60-69	0.67	0.72	0.84	0.87	0.82
70-79	0.99	1.17	1.32	1.46	0.93
80+	1.65	2.22	(1.84)	2.11	(2.64)

Environmental Factors

Driver Age	Light Conditions					Weather Conditions	
	Daylight	Dark	Dark, lighted	Dawn	Dusk	Normal	Rain/sleet/ Snow/fog/etc.
<20	1.97	1.67	1.66	2.70	2.11	1.88	2.13
20-29	1.25	1.14	1.11	1.52	1.10	1.21	1.29
30-39	0.84	0.88	0.83	0.78	0.73	0.84	0.83
40-49	0.72	0.69	0.73	0.53	0.73	0.72	0.70
50-59	0.66	0.66	0.75	0.79	0.75	0.69	0.59
60-69	0.71	0.73	0.83	0.60	0.97	0.73	0.68
70-79	1.11	1.25	1.23	(4.46)	1.47	1.17	0.90
80+	1.84	4.22	2.43	(8.57)	2.80	1.93	1.71

Specific Circumstances

Driver Age	2-Lanes			3-4 Lanes		5+ Lanes		Interstate	
	<= 35 mph	40-45 mph	50-55 mph	40-45 mph	50-55 mph	40-45 mph	50+ mph	<65 mph	65+ mph
<20	1.81	2.12	2.11	2.00	1.82	1.81	2.48	2.11	2.73
20-29	1.17	1.20	1.18	1.17	1.28	1.18	1.21	1.32	1.41
30-39	0.82	0.72	0.87	0.83	0.93	0.89	0.84	0.94	0.84
40-49	0.72	0.71	0.69	0.72	0.70	0.69	0.68	0.69	0.76
50-59	0.74	0.72	0.61	0.72	0.77	0.68	0.74	0.66	0.56
60-69	0.81	0.67	0.64	0.74	0.61	0.60	0.67	0.66	0.68
70-79	1.01	1.30	1.42	1.19	1.31	1.44	0.65	0.91	0.56
80+	1.29	1.47	3.00	1.92	(0.91)**	2.40	6.34	(3.79)	(2.38)

** Raw count 46/23

At-Fault Vehicle Maneuver and Traffic Control Device

Driver Age	Going Straight				Turning Left				Turning Right		
	Signal	Flash.	Stop	Yield	Signal	Flash.	Stop	Yield	Signal	Stop	Yield
<20	2.06	2.05	1.86	1.81	1.72	2.10	1.88	1.72	1.53	1.82	1.52
20-29	1.40	1.28	1.16	1.44	1.01	0.89	1.06	0.56	1.10	1.09	1.61
30-39	0.90	0.82	0.82	0.86	0.69	0.81	0.75	0.64	0.63	0.59	0.89
40-49	0.68	0.85	0.65	0.69	0.65	1.17	0.67	0.34	0.99	0.72	0.37
50-59	0.70	0.65	0.70	0.57	0.79	0.53	0.71	2.16	0.55	0.94	(0.35)
60-69	0.59	0.64	0.88	1.40	1.05	(0.92)	0.83	(1.48)	1.11	1.15	(0.98)
70-79	0.81	(0.79)	1.50	0.70	2.32	(2.61)	1.48	(2.08)	1.85	1.37	(1.45)
80+	1.66	(1.60)	2.28	(2.10)	3.11	(3.20)	2.05	(1.10)	(4.82)	(1.27)	(3.48)

REFERENCES

[1]   Braitman, K. A., Kirley, B. B., Ferguson, S. & Chaudhary, N. K. (2007). Factors leading to older drivers' intersection crashes. *Traffic Injury Prevention, 8(3)*, 267-74.

[2]   Chandraratn, S. & Stamatiadis, N. (2003). Problem driving maneuvers of elderly drivers. *Transportation Research Record, 1843*, 89-95.

[3]   Garber, N. J. & Srinivasan, R. (1991). Characteristics of accidents involving elderly drivers at intersections. *Transportation Research Record, 1325*, 8-16.

[4]   Langford, J. & Koppel, S. (2006). Epidemiology of older driver crashes – identifying older driver risk factors and exposure patterns. *Transportation Research Part F, 9*, 309-321.

[5]   Langford, J., Koppel, S., Andrea, D. & Fildes, B. (2006). Determining older driver crash responsibility from police and insurance data. *Traffic Injury Prevention, 7*, 343-451.

[6]   Mayhew, D. R., Simpson, H. M. & Ferguson, S. A. (2006). Collisions involving senior drivers: high-risk conditions and locations. *Traffic Injury Prevention, 7(2)*, 117-124.

[7]   McGwin, G., Jr. & Brown, D. B. (1999). Characteristics of traffic crashes among young, middle- aged, and older drivers. *Accident Analysis and Prevention, 31*, 181-198.

[8]   Oxley, J., Fildes, B., Corben, B. & Langford, J. (2006). Intersection design for older drivers. *Transportation Research Part F*, 335-346.

[9]   Reinfurt, D. W., Stewart, J. R., Stutts, J. C. & Rodgman, E. A. (2000). *Investigations of Crashes and Casualties Associated with Older Drivers.*

Report prepared for General Motors Corporation and the U.S. Department of Transportation. Chapel Hill, NC: University of North Carolina (Highway Safety Research Center). Available at http://www.hsrc.unc.edu/research_library/PDFs/investigations2000.pdf

[10] Staplin, L. & Lyles, R. W. (1991). Age differences in motion perception and specific traffic maneuver problems. *Transportation Research Record, 1325*, 23-3 3.

[11] Staplin, L., Gish, K. & Wagner, E. (2003). MaryPODS revisited: Updated crash analysis and implications for screening program implementation. *Journal of Safety Research, 34(4)*, 389-397.

In: Crash Risks and Safety Issues Among...   ISBN: 978-1-61209-348-2
Editor: William E. Madsen   © 2011 Nova Science Publishers, Inc.

Chapter 2

OLDER DRIVER SAFETY: KNOWLEDGE SHARING SHOULD HELP STATES PREPARE FOR INCREASE IN OLDER DRIVER POPULATION

United States Government Accountability Office

WHY GAO DID THIS STUDY

As people age, their physical, visual, and cognitive abilities may decline, making it more difficult for them to drive safely. Older drivers are also more likely to suffer injuries or die in crashes than drivers in other age groups (see fig.). These safety issues will increase in significance because older adults represent the fastest- growing U.S. population segment.

GAO examined (1) what the federal government has done to promote practices to make roads safer for older drivers and the extent to which states have implemented those practices, (2) the extent to which states assess the fitness of older drivers and what support the federal government has provided, and (3) what initiatives selected states have implemented to improve the safety of older drivers. To conduct this study, GAO surveyed 51 state departments of transportation (DOT), visited six states, and interviewed federal transportation officials.

WHAT GAO RECOMMENDS

GAO is recommending that the Secretary of Transportation direct the FHWA and NHTSA Administrators to implement a mechanism to allow states to share information on older driver safety practices. The Department of Health and Human Services agreed with the report. The Department of Transportation provided technical corrections but did not offer overall comments on the report.

WHAT GAO FOUND

The Federal Highway Administration (FHWA) has recommended practices— such as using larger letters on signs—targeted to making roadways easier for older drivers to navigate. FHWA also provides funding that states may use for projects that address older driver safety. States have, to varying degrees, adopted FHWA's recommended practices. For example, 24 states reported including about half or more of FHWA's practices in state design guides, while the majority of states reported implementing certain FHWA practices in roadway construction, operations, and maintenance activities. States generally do not place high priority on projects that specifically address older driver safety but try to include practices that benefit older drivers in all projects.

More than half of the states have implemented licensing requirements for older drivers that are more stringent than requirements for younger drivers, but states' assessment practices are not comprehensive. For example, these practices primarily involve more frequent or in-person renewals and mandatory vision screening but do not generally include assessments of physical and cognitive functions. While requirements for in-person license renewals generally appear to correspond with lower crash rates for drivers over age 85, the validity of other assessment tools is less clear. The National Highway Traffic Safety Administration (NHTSA) is sponsoring research and other initiatives to develop and assist states in implementing more comprehensive driver fitness assessment practices.

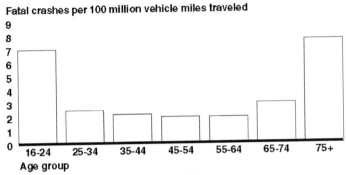

Sources: GAO analysis of NHTSA and USDOT data.

Fatal Crashes by Driver Age Group per 100 Million Vehicle Miles Traveled (2001)

Five of the six states GAO visited have implemented coordination groups to assemble a broad range of stakeholders to develop strategies and foster efforts to improve older driver safety in areas of strategic planning, education and awareness, licensing and driver fitness assessment, roadway engineering, and data analysis. However, knowledge sharing among states on older driver safety initiatives is limited, and officials said states could benefit from knowledge of other states' initiatives.

ABBREVIATIONS

AAMVA	American Association of Motor Vehicle Administrators
AASHTO	American Association of State and Highway Transportation Officials
AOA	Administration on Aging
CTRE	Center for Transportation Research and Education
DHSMV	Department of Highway Safety and Motor Vehicles
DOT	Department of Transportation
FADC	Florida At-Risk Driver Council
FHWA	Federal Highway Administration
GHSA	Governors Highway Safety Association
HSIP	Highway Safety Improvement Program
IDOT	Iowa Department of Transportation
LTAP	Local Technical Assistance Program
MAB	Medical Advisory Board
MDDB	Mature Driver Database

MPO	Metropolitan Planning Organization
MUTCD	*Manual on Uniform Traffic Control Devices*
NCHRP	National Cooperative Highway Research Program
NHTSA	National Highway Traffic Safety Administration
NIA	National Institute on Aging
OCTS	Older Californian Traffic Safety Task Force
ODMVS	Oregon Driver and Motor Vehicle Services
SAFETEA-LU	Safe, Accountable, Flexible, Efficient Transportation Equity Act: A Legacy for Users
SEMCOG	Southeast Michigan Council of Governments
SHSP	Strategic Highway Safety Plan
STIP	Statewide Transportation Improvement Program

April 11, 2007

The Honorable Herb Kohl
Chairman
The Honorable Gordon H. Smith
Ranking Minority Member
Special Committee on Aging
United States Senate

As people age, their physical, visual, and cognitive abilities may deteriorate, making it more difficult for them to drive safely. Furthermore, older drivers are more likely to suffer injuries or die in accidents than drivers in most other age groups, in part because of the greater frailty that comes with age. Older driver safety issues will become increasingly significant in the future because older adults represent the fastest-growing segment of the U.S. population—by 2030 the number of licensed drivers aged 65 and older is expected to nearly double to about 57 million. Consequently, efforts to build safer roads and develop better methods of assessing driver fitness are keys to helping older people continue to drive safely and maintain their mobility, independence, and health.

Concerned about the safety of older drivers, you requested that we review steps being taken by both the federal and state governments to support older driver safety initiatives. Accordingly, this report addresses (1) what the federal government has done to promote practices to make roads safer for older drivers and the extent to which states have implemented those practices, (2) the extent to which states assess the fitness of older drivers and what support the federal government has provided, and (3) what initiatives selected states have implemented to improve the safety of older drivers.

To determine what the federal government has done to promote practices to make roads safer for older drivers, we reviewed documents and interviewed officials from the Federal Highway Administration (FHWA) within the U.S. Department of Transportation (DOT). To obtain information on the extent to which states are implementing these practices, we surveyed and received responses from DOTs in each of the 50 states and the District of Columbia.[1] This report does not contain all the results from the survey. The survey and a more complete tabulation of the results can be viewed at www.gao.gov/cgi-bin/getrpt?GAO. To determine the extent to which states assess the fitness of older drivers and what support the federal government has provided, we reviewed documents and interviewed officials from the National Highway Traffic Safety Administration (NHTSA) within the U.S. DOT, the National Institute on Aging (NIA) and the Administration on Aging (AOA) within the U.S. Department of Health and Human Services (HHS), and the American Association of Motor Vehicle Administrators (AAMVA)—a nongovernmental organization that represents state driver licensing agencies. To obtain information on initiatives that selected states have implemented, we conducted case studies in six states—California, Florida, Iowa, Maryland, Michigan, and Oregon—that transportation experts identified as progressive in their efforts to improve older driver safety. The scope of our work focused on older driver safety. Prior GAO work addressed the associated issue of senior mobility for those who do not drive.[2] We conducted our work from April 2006 through April 2007 in accordance with generally accepted government auditing standards. (For details of our objectives, scope, and methodology, see app. I.)

RESULTS IN BRIEF

To make roads safer for older drivers, FHWA has recommended practices—such as using larger letters on signs, placing advance street name signs before intersections, and improving intersection layouts—for the design and operation of roadways that make them easier for older drivers to navigate. FHWA is also continuing research to demonstrate the effectiveness of these practices. While these practices are designed to address older drivers' needs, their implementation can make roads safer for all drivers. States have, to varying degrees, incorporated FHWA's older driver safety practices into their design standards, implemented the practices in roadway operation and maintenance activities, trained technical staff in applying the practices, and coordinated with local agencies to promote the use of the practices. Following are the actions taken by the 51 DOTs we surveyed in the states and District of Columbia:

- 24 states reported including about half, most, almost all, or all of FHWA's practices in their state design guides.
- 51 states reported implementing advance traffic control warning signage on approaches to intersections.
- 12 states reported they had trained about half, most, almost all, or all of their technical staff.
- 38 states reported they had held sessions on older driver issues with local governments.

FHWA also provides federal highway funding that states may use to implement projects that address older driver safety. While older driver safety projects are eligible for federal highway funding, state DOTs generally place a higher priority on and commit more of their limited resources to other projects—such as railway/highway intersection safety projects, roadside hazard elimination or mitigation projects, road intersection safety projects, and roadway departure projects—that more broadly affect all drivers. Although older driver safety is not the primary focus of these projects, the projects may incorporate FHWA's recommended practices to improve older driver safety.

More than half of the states have implemented assessment practices to support licensing requirements for older drivers that are more stringent than requirements for younger drivers. These requirements generally involve more frequent renewals (16 states), mandatory vision screening (10 states), in-person renewals (5 states), and mandatory road tests (2 states) for older drivers. In addition, all states accept physician reports and third-party referrals of concerns about drivers, while 36 states use medical advisory boards to assist licensing agencies in assessing driver fitness. However, assessment of driver fitness in all states is not comprehensive because cognitive and physical functions are generally not evaluated to the same extent as visual functions. Furthermore, the effectiveness of assessment practices used by states is largely unknown. For example, research indicates that in-person license renewal is associated with lower accident rates for older drivers—particularly for those aged 85 and older— but vision screening, road tests, and more frequent license renewal cycles are not always associated with lower older driver fatality rates.

Because there is insufficient evidence on the validity and reliability of driver fitness assessments, states may have difficulty discerning which assessments to implement. Recognizing the need for better assessment tools, NHTSA is developing more comprehensive practices to assess driver fitness and intends to provide technical assistance to states in implementing these practices.

A key initiative implemented in five of the six states we visited was their use of coordination groups to assemble a broad range of stakeholders—including public agencies, academic institutions, medical professionals, and partner nongovernmental organizations—to develop strategies and implement efforts to improve older driver safety. Specific efforts under way in the states we visited were generally in areas of strategic planning, education and awareness, licensing and driver fitness assessment, engineering, and data analysis. Following are examples:

- Florida promotes education and public awareness through the Florida GrandDriver® Program that reaches out to older drivers by providing Web-based information related to driver safety courses and alternative transportation; provides training to medical, social service, and transportation professionals on older driver issues; sponsors safety talks at senior centers; and holds events to help older drivers determine if they need to make adjustments to better fit in their cars.
- Michigan conducted a demonstration program, funded jointly by state, county, and local government agencies, along with AAA Michigan, that made low-cost improvements at over 300 high-risk, signal-controlled intersections in the Detroit area; an evaluation of 30 of these intersections indicated that the injury rate for older drivers was reduced by more than twice as much as for drivers aged 25 to 64 years.

However, according to officials we spoke with in these six states, knowledge sharing among states on older driver safety practices is limited, and the general consensus of these officials is that states could benefit from knowledge of other states' initiatives to address older driver safety issues. According to these officials, sharing this information could help them make decisions about whether to implement new practices and identifying the research basis for practices could assist them in assessing the benefits to be derived from implementing a particular practice. To facilitate this transfer of knowledge between stakeholders in all states, we are recommending that the Secretary of Transportation implement a mechanism that would allow states to share information on leading practices for enhancing the safety of older drivers. This mechanism could also include information on other initiatives and guidance, such as FHWA's research on the effectiveness of road design practices and NHTSA's research on more effective driver assessment practices.

We provided a draft of this report to the Department of Health and Human Services and to the Department of Transportation for review and comment.

The Department of Health and Human Services agreed with the report and offered technical suggestions which we have incorporated, as appropriate. (See app. III for the Department of Health and Human Services' written comments.) The Department of Transportation did not offer overall comments on the report or its recommendation. The department did offer several technical comments, which we incorporated where appropriate.

BACKGROUND

Driving is a complex task that depends on visual, cognitive, and physical functions that enable a person to

- see traffic and road conditions;
- recognize what is seen, process the information, and decide how to react; and
- physically act to control the vehicle.

Although the aging process affects people at different rates and in different ways, functional declines associated with aging can affect driving ability. For example, vision declines may reduce the ability to see other vehicles, traffic signals, signs, lane markings, and pedestrians; cognitive declines may reduce the ability to recognize traffic conditions, remember destinations, and make appropriate decisions in operating the vehicle; and physical declines may reduce the ability to perform movements required to control the vehicle.

A particular concern is older drivers with dementia, often as a result of illnesses such as Alzheimer's disease. Dementia impairs cognitive and sensory functions causing disorientation, potentially leading to dangerous driving practices. Age is the most significant risk factor for developing dementia—approximately 12 percent of those aged 65 to 84 are likely to develop the condition while over 47 percent of those aged 85 and older are likely to be afflicted. For drivers with the condition, the risk of being involved in a crash is two to eight times greater than for those with no cognitive impairment. However, some drivers with dementia, particularly in the early stages, may still be capable of driving safely.

Older drivers experience fewer fatal crashes per licensed driver compared with drivers in younger age groups; however, on the basis of miles driven, older drivers have a comparatively higher involvement in fatal crashes. Over the past decade, the rate of older driver involvement in fatal crashes, measured on the basis of licensed drivers, has decreased and, overall, older drivers have a lower rate of fatal crashes than drivers in younger age groups (see figure 1). Older drivers' fatal crash rate per licensed driver is lower than corresponding rates for drivers in younger age groups, in part, because older drivers drive fewer miles per year than younger drivers, may hold licenses even though they no longer drive, and may avoid driving during times and under conditions when crashes tend to occur, such as during rush hour or at night. However, on the basis of miles traveled, older drivers who are involved in a crash are more likely to suffer fatal injuries than are drivers in younger age groups who are involved in crashes. As shown in figure 2, drivers aged 65 to 74 are more likely to be involved in a fatal crash than all but the youngest drivers (aged 16 to 24), and drivers aged 75 and older are more likely than drivers in all other age groups to be involved in a fatal crash.

Older drivers will be increasingly exposed to crash risks because older adults are the fastest-growing segment of the U.S. population, and future generations of older drivers are expected to drive more miles per year and at older ages compared with the current older-driver cohort. The U.S. Census Bureau projects that the population of adults aged 65 and older will more than double, from 35.1 million people (12.4 percent of total population) in 2000 to 86.7 million people (20.7 percent of total population) in 2050 (see figure 3).

Intersections pose a particular safety problem for older drivers. Navigating through intersections requires the ability to make rapid decisions, react quickly, and accurately judge speed and distance. As these abilities can diminish through aging, older drivers have more difficulties at intersections and are more likely to be involved in a fatal crash at these locations. Research shows that 37 percent of traffic-related fatalities involving drivers aged 65 and older occur at intersections compared with 18 percent for drivers aged 26 to 64.[3] Figure 4 illustrates how fatalities at intersections represent an increasing proportion of all traffic fatalities as drivers age.

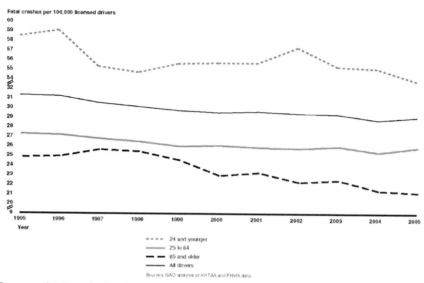

Sources: GAO analysis of NHTSA and FHWA data.

Figure 1. Drivers in Fatal Crashes per 100,000 Licensed Drivers (1995 to 2005)

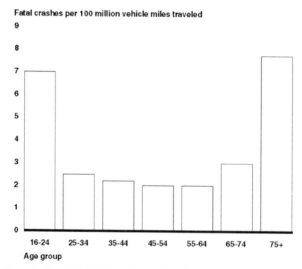

Sources: GAO analysis of NHTSA and USDOT data.

Note: 2001 is the most recent year for which age based data on vehicle miles traveled
is available.

Figure 2. Fatal Crashes by Driver Age Group per 100 Million Vehicle Miles Traveled
(2001)

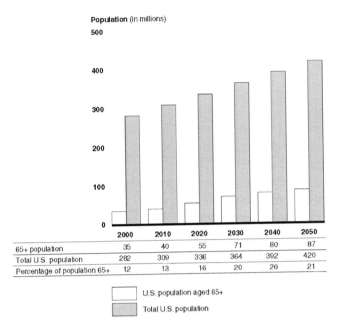

	2000	2010	2020	2030	2040	2050
65+ population	35	40	55	71	80	87
Total U.S. population	282	309	336	364	392	420
Percentage of population 65+	12	13	16	20	20	21

Source: GAO presentation of U.S. Census Bureau data.

Figure 3. Population Growth of Adults Aged 65 and Older

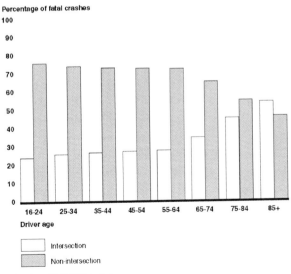

Source: GAO analysis of NHTSA data.

Figure 4. Fatal Crashes at Intersections by Driver Age (2004)

DOT—through FHWA and NHTSA—has a role in promoting older driver safety, although states are directly responsible for operating their roadways and establishing driver licensing requirements. FHWA focuses on roadway engineering and has established guidelines for designers to use in developing engineering enhancements to roadways to accommodate the declining functional capabilities of older drivers. NHTSA focuses on reducing traffic-related injuries and fatalities among older people by promoting, in conjunction with nongovernmental organizations, research, education, and programs aimed at identifying older drivers with functional limitations that impair driving performance. NHTSA has developed several guides, brochures, and booklets for use by the medical community, law enforcement officials, older drivers' family members, and older drivers themselves that provide guidance on what actions can be taken to improve older drivers' capabilities or to compensate for lost capabilities. Additionally, NIA supports research related to older driver safety through administering grants designed to examine, among other issues, how impairments in sensory and cognitive functions impact driving ability.

These federal initiatives support state efforts to make roads safer for older drivers and establish assessment practices to evaluate the fitness of older drivers.

The Safe, Accountable, Flexible, Efficient Transportation Equity Act: A Legacy for Users (SAFETEA-LU),[4] signed into law in August 2005, establishes a framework for federal investment in transportation and has specific provisions for older driver safety. SAFETEA-LU authorizes $193.1 billion in Federal-Aid Highway Program funds to be distributed through FHWA for states to implement road preservation, improvement, and construction projects, some of which may include improvements for older drivers. SAFETEA-LU also directs DOT to carry out a program to improve traffic signs and pavement markings to accommodate older drivers. To fulfill these requirements, FHWA has updated or plans to update its guidebooks on highway design for older drivers, plans to conduct workshops on designing roads for older drivers that will be available to state practitioners, and has added a senior mobility series to its bimonthly magazine that highlights advances and innovations in highway/traffic research and technology. Additionally, SAFTEA-LU authorizes NHTSA to spend $1.7 million per year (during fiscal years 2006 through 2009) in establishing a comprehensive research and demonstration program to improve traffic safety for older drivers.[5]

FHWA HAS RECOMMENDED PRACTICES AND MADE FUNDING AVAILABLE TO MAKE ROADS SAFER FOR OLDER DRIVERS, BUT STATES GENERALLY GIVE HIGHER PRIORITY TO OTHER SAFETY ISSUES

FHWA has recommended practices for designing and operating roadways to make them safer for older drivers and administers SAFETEA-LU funds that states—which own and operate most roadways under state or local government authority—may use for road maintenance or construction projects to improve roads for older drivers. To varying degrees, states are implementing FHWA's older driver practices and developing plans and programs that consider older drivers' needs. However, responses to our survey indicated that other safety issues—such as railway and highway intersections and roadside hazard elimination—are of greater concern to states, and states generally place a higher priority on projects that address these issues rather than projects targeted only towards older drivers.

FHWA HAS RECOMMENDED ROAD DESIGN AND OPERATING PRACTICES AND FUNDS PROGRAMS TO IMPROVE OLDER DRIVER SAFETY

FHWA has issued guidelines and recommendations to states on practices that are intended to make roads safer for older drivers, such as the *Highway Design Handbook for Older Drivers and Pedestrians.*[6] The practices emphasize cost-effective construction and maintenance measures involving both the physical layout of the roadway and use of traffic control devices such as signs, pavement markings, and traffic signals.[7] The practices are specifically designed to improve conditions at sites—intersections, interchanges, curved roads, construction work zones, and railroad crossings— known to be unsafe for older drivers. While these practices are designed to address older drivers' needs, implementation of these practices can make roads safer for all drivers.

- *Intersections*—Recognizing that intersections are particularly problematic for older drivers, FHWA's top priority in its *Highway Design Handbook for Older Drivers and Pedestrians* is intersection improvements. Practices to improve older drivers' ability to navigate intersections include using bigger signs with larger lettering to identify street names, consistent placement of lane use signs and arrow pavement markings, aligning lanes to improve drivers' ability to see oncoming traffic, and using reflective markers on medians and island curbs at intersections to make them easier to see at night. See figures 5 through 8 for these and additional intersection improvement practices.

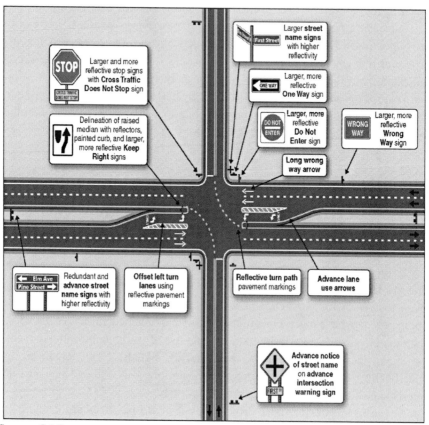

Source: GAO.

Figure 5. Older Driver Improvements at an Intersection

Sources: Michigan DOT, FHWA, and GAO.

Figure 6. Examples of Improved Signs and Ability to See Oncoming Traffic

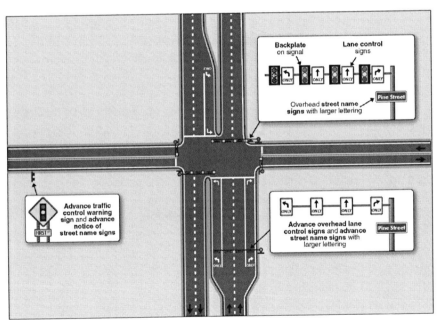

Source: GAO.

Figure 7. Older Driver Improvements at an Intersection with Traffic Signals

- *Interchanges*—Practices to aid older drivers at interchanges include using signs and pavement markings to better identify right and wrong directions of travel and configuring on-ramps to provide a longer distance for accelerating and merging into traffic. See figure 9 for these and additional interchange improvement practices.

- *Road curves*—Practices to assist older drivers on curves include using signs and reflective markers—especially on tight curves—to clearly delineate the path of the road. See figure 10 for these and additional curve improvement practices.

- *Construction work zones*—Practices to improve older driver safety in construction work zones include increasing the length of time messages are visible on changeable message signs; providing easily discernable barriers between opposing traffic lanes in crossovers; using properly sized devices (cones and drums) to delineate temporary lanes; and installing temporary reflective pavement markers to make lanes easier to navigate at night.

- *Railroad crossings*—Practices to help older drivers are aimed at making the railroad crossing more conspicuous by using reflective materials on the front and back of railroad crossing signs and delineating the approach to the crossing with reflective posts. See figure 11 for these and additional railroad crossing improvement practices.

FHWA is continuing to research and develop practices to make roads safer for older drivers. FHWA also promotes the implementation of these practices by sponsoring studies and demonstration projects, updating its *Highway Design Handbook for Older Drivers and Pedestrians*, and training state and local transportation officials. For example, FHWA is supporting a research study—to be conducted over the next 3 to 5 years— on the effectiveness of selected low-cost road improvements in reducing the number and severity of crashes for all drivers.[8] With the findings of this and other studies, FHWA plans to update its guidelines to refine existing or recommend new practices in improving older driver safety. In addition, FHWA is considering changes to its MUTCD—to be published in 2009—that will enhance older driver safety by updating standards related to sign legibility and traffic signal visibility.

Under SAFETEA-LU, FHWA provides funding that states may use to implement highway maintenance or construction projects that can enhance older driver safety.[9] However, because projects to enhance older driver safety can be developed under several different SAFETEA-LU programs, it is difficult to determine the amount of federal funding dedicated to highway improvements for older drivers. While older driver safety is generally not the primary focus of projects funded through SAFETEA-LU programs, improvements made to roads may incorporate elements of FHWA's older driver safety practices. For example, under SAFETEA-LU's Highway Safety

Improvement Program (HSIP), states submit a Strategicv Highway Safety Plan (SHSP)[10] after reviewing crash and other data and determining what areas need to be emphasized when making safety improvements. If older driver safety is found to be an area of emphasis, a state may develop projects to be funded under the HSIP that provide, for example, improved traffic signs, pavement markings, and road layouts consistent with practices listed in FHWA's *Highway Design Handbook for Older Drivers and Pedestrians*.

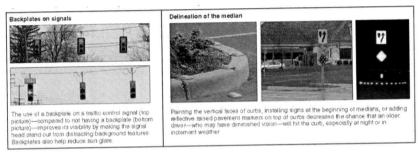

Sources: Iowa DOT, FHWA, and GAO.

Figure 8. Examples of Improved Signals and Median Markings

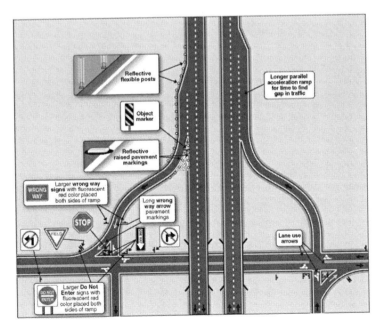

Figure 9. Older Driver Improvements at an Interchange

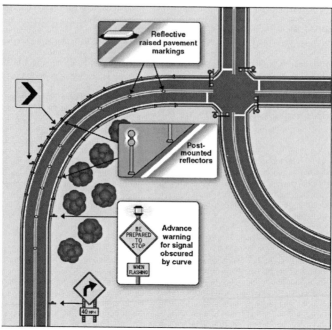

Source: GAO.

Figure 10. Older Driver Improvements on Curves

Some States have Implemented FHWA's Recommended Practices and Considered Older Drivers in Highway Safety Plans and Programs, but Other Safety Issues Generally Receive Greater Priority

State DOTs have, to varying degrees, incorporated FHWA's older driver safety practices into their design standards; implemented the practices in construction, operations, and maintenance activities; trained technical staff in applying the practices; and coordinated with local agencies to promote the use of the practices. The states' responses to our survey indicate the range in states' efforts.

Design standards. Nearly half of the states have incorporated about half or more of FHWA's practices into their design standards, as follows:[11]

- 24 state DOTs reported including about half, most, almost all, or all of the recommendations.
- 20 reported including some of the recommendations.
- 6 reported including few or none of the recommendations.

Construction, operations, and maintenance activities. Even though most state DOTs have not incorporated all FHWA practices into their design standards, the majority of states have implemented some FHWA practices in construction, operations, and maintenance activities, particularly in the areas of intersections and work zones (see table 1).

Table 1. Most Widely Implemented Practices Recommended by FHWA for Improving Older Driver Safety

FHWA practice	Number of states that have implemented the practice
Advance "STOP AHEAD," "YIELD AHEAD," and "SIGNAL AHEAD" signs on approaches to intersections when existing signs or signals are not visible soon enough for drivers to respond appropriately	51
Channelizing devices such as traffic cones, tubular markers, striped panel signs, drums, or temporary barriers to separate opposing traffic in construction zones to provide conspicuous and unambiguous traffic control	48
Dashed turn path pavement markings in intersections where evidence suggests that older drivers may have difficulty negotiating turns	41
Overhead lane control signs at intersections with traffic signals where drivers may have trouble positioning themselves in the correct lane	40
Reflective devices on medians and island curbs at intersections to make them more obvious	39

Source: State DOT responses to GAO survey.

Note: In our questionnaire, we asked state officials whether they had implemented 14 specific recommendations. Six of those recommendations were selected from the 136 recommendations found in *FHWA's Highway Design Handbook for Older Drivers and Pedestrians* (2001). The 8 remaining recommendations were chosen from the 35 similar recommendations cited in *FHWA's Travel Better, Travel Longer: A Pocket Guide to Improve Traffic Control and Mobility for Our Older Population* (2003).

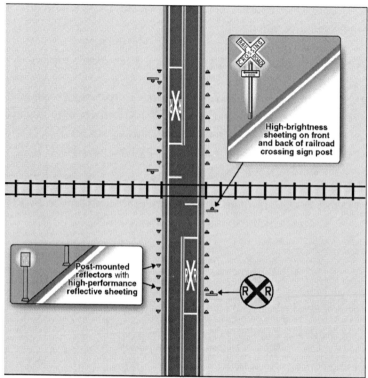

Source: GAO.

Figure 11. Older Driver Improvements at Railroad Crossings

Training. Nearly one-fourth of state DOTs have provided training on FHWA practices to half or more of their technical staff, as follows:

- 12 state DOTs reported having trained about half, most, almost all, or all of their technical staff.
- 32 have trained some of their technical staff.
- 7 have trained few or none of their technical staff.

Coordination with local agencies. Because state transportation agencies do not own local roads—which may account for the majority of roads in a state[12]—coordination with local governments is important in promoting older driver safety in the design, operation, and maintenance of local roads. The states reported using a variety of methods in their work with local governments to improve older driver safety (see table 2).

Table 2. Methods Reported by States for Working with Local Governments to Improve Older Driver Safety

Method used	Number of states using method
Holding sessions at statewide conferences	38
Offering training in road design and traffic control	32
Developing programs with the Local Technical Assistance Program[a](LTAP)	29
Developing programs with Metropolitan Planning Organizations[b](MPO)	21

Source: State DOT responses to GAO survey.

[a] LTAP is an FHWA program that enables local highway agencies to access technology designed to help them meet growing demands placed on local roads, bridges, and public transportation systems. Through LTAP, a nationwide system of technology transfer centers—placed in locations such as universities and state highway agencies—has been established to facilitate information sharing. Sources of funding for LTAP include FHWA, state DOTs, local agencies, and universities.

[b] An MPO is a transportation policy-making organization made up of representatives from local government and transportation authorities. Federal highway and transit statutes require, as a condition for spending federal highway or transit funds in urbanized areas, the designation of MPOs that are responsible for planning, programming, and coordinating federal highway and transit investments.

Table 3. Types of Safety Projects in Which States Report Investing Resources to a Great or Very Great Extent

Type of safety project	Number of states investing to a great or very great extent
Roadside hazard elimination or mitigation projects	36
Road intersection safety projects	36
Safety projects at railway/highway intersections	35
Roadway departure projects	35
Older driver safety projects	2

Source: State DOT responses to GAO survey.

States also varied in their efforts to consult stakeholders on older driver issues in developing highway safety plans (defined in the state SHSP) and lists of projects in their Statewide Transportation Improvement Programs (STIP).[13] According to our survey, 27 of the 51 state DOTs have established older driver safety as a component of their SHSPs, and our survey indicated that, in developing their SHSPs, these states were more likely to consult with stakeholders concerned about older driver safety than were states that did not include an older driver component in their plans. Obtaining input from stakeholders concerned about older driver safety—from both governmental and nongovernmental organizations—is important because they can contribute additional information, and can sometimes provide resources, to address older driver safety issues. For example, elderly mobility was identified by the Michigan State Safety Commission to be an emerging issue and, in February 1998, funded the Southeast Michigan Council of Governments (SEMCOG) to convene a statewide, interdisciplinary Elderly Mobility and Safety Task Force. SEMCOG coordinated with various stakeholder groups—Michigan DOT, Michigan Department of State, Michigan Office of Highway Safety Planning, Michigan Department of Community Health, Office of Services to the Aging, University of Michigan Transportation Research Institute, agencies on aging, and AAA Michigan among others—in developing a statewide plan to address older driver safety and mobility issues.[14] This plan—which outlines recommendations in the areas of traffic engineering, alternative transportation, housing and land use, health and medicine, licensing, and education and awareness—forms the basis for the strategy defined in Michigan's SHSP to address older drivers' mobility and safety.

Even though 27 state DOTs have reported establishing older driver safety as a component of their SHSPs, only 4 state DOTs reported including older driver safety improvement projects in their fiscal year 2007 STIPs. However, state STIPs may contain projects that will benefit older drivers. For example, 49 state DOTs reported including funding for intersection improvements in their STIPs. Because drivers are increasingly more likely to be involved in an intersection crash as they age, older drivers, in particular, should benefit from states' investments in intersection safety projects,[15] which generally provide improved signage, traffic signals, turning lanes, and other features consistent with FHWA's older driver safety practices.

Although older driver safety could become a more pressing need in the future as the population of older drivers increases, states are applying their resources to areas that pose greater safety concerns. In response to a question in our survey about the extent to which resources—defined to include staff hours and funds spent on research, professional services, and construction contracts—were invested in different types of safety projects, many state DOTs indicated that they apply resources to a great or very great extent to safety projects other than those concerning older driver safety (see table 3).[16]

Survey responses indicated that resource constraints are a significant contributing factor to limiting states' implementation of FHWA's older driver safety practices and development of strategic plans and programs that consider older driver concerns.

MORE THAN HALF OF STATES HAVE IMPLEMENTED SOME ASSESSMENT PRACTICES FOR OLDER DRIVERS, AND NHTSA IS SPONSORING RESEARCH TO DEVELOP MORE COMPREHENSIVE ASSESSMENTS

More than half of state licensing agencies have implemented assessment practices to support licensing requirements for older drivers that are more stringent than requirements for younger drivers.[17] These requirements—established under state licensing procedures—generally involve more frequent renewals (16 states), mandatory vision screening (10 states), in- person renewals (5 states) and mandatory road tests (2 states). However, assessment of driver fitness in all states is not comprehensive because cognitive and physical functions are generally not evaluated to the same extent as visual function. Furthermore, the effectiveness of assessment practices used by states is largely unknown. Recognizing the need for better assessment tools, NHTSA is developing more comprehensive practices to assess driver fitness and intends to provide technical assistance to states in implementing these practices.

Over Half of the States Have More Stringent Licensing Requirements for Older Drivers, but Assessment Practices Are Not Comprehensive

Over half of the states have procedures that establish licensing requirements for older drivers that are more stringent than requirements for younger drivers. These requirements generally include more frequent license renewal, mandatory vision screening, in-person renewals, and mandatory road tests. In addition, states may also consider input from medical advisory boards, physician reports, and third-party referrals in assessing driver fitness and making licensing decisions. (See figure 12 and app. II for additional details.)

- *Accelerated renewal*—Sixteen states have accelerated renewal cycles for older drivers that require drivers older than a specific age to renew their licenses more frequently. Colorado, for example, normally requires drivers to renew their licenses every 10 years, but drivers aged 61 and older must renew their licenses every 5 years.

- *Vision screening*—Ten states require older drivers to undergo vision assessments, conducted by either the Department of Motor Vehicles or their doctor, as part of the license renewal process. These assessments generally test for visual acuity or sharpness of vision.[18] For example, the average age for mandatory vision screening is 62, with some states beginning this screening as early as age 40 (Maine and Maryland) and other states beginning as late as age 80 (Florida and Virginia).

- *In-person renewal*—Five states—Alaska, Arizona, California, Colorado, and Louisiana—that otherwise allow license renewal by mail require older drivers to renew their licenses in person. Arizona, California, and Louisiana do not permit mail renewal for drivers aged 70 and older. Alaska does not allow mail renewal for drivers aged 69 and older, while Colorado requires in-person renewal for those over age 61.

- *Road test*—Two states, New Hampshire and Illinois, require older drivers to pass road examinations upon reaching 75 years and at all subsequent renewals.

In addition, states have adopted other practices to assist licensing agencies in assessing driver fitness and identifying older drivers whose driving fitness may need to be reevaluated.

- *Medical Advisory Boards*—Thirty-five states and the District of Columbia rely on Medical Advisory Boards (MAB) to assist licensing agencies in evaluating people with medical conditions or functional limitations that may affect their ability to drive. A MAB may be organizationally placed within a state's transportation, public safety, or motor vehicle department. Board members—practicing physicians or health care professionals—are typically nominated or appointed by the state medical association, motor vehicle administrator, or governor's office. Some MABs review individual cases typically compiled by case workers who collect and review medical and other evidence such as accident reports that is used to make a determination about a person's fitness to drive. The volume of cases reviewed by MABs varies greatly across states. For example, seven state MABs review more than 1,000 cases annually, while another seven MABs review fewer than 10 cases annually.

- *Physician reports*—While all states accept reports of potentially unsafe drivers from physicians, nine states require physicians to report physical conditions that might impair driving skills. For example, California specifically requires doctors to report a diagnosis of Alzheimer's disease or related disorders, including dementia, while Delaware, New Jersey, and Nevada require physicians to report cases of epilepsy and those involving a person's loss of consciousness. However, not all states assure physicians that such reports will be kept confidential, so physicians may choose not to report patients if they fear retribution in the form of a lawsuit or loss of the patient's business.

- *Third-party referrals*—In addition to reports from physicians, all states accept third-party referrals of concerns about drivers of any age. Upon receipt of the referral, the licensing agency may choose to contact the driver in question to assess the person's fitness to drive. A recent survey of state licensing agencies found that nearly three-fourths of all referrals came from law enforcement officials (37 percent) and physicians or other medical professionals (35 percent). About 13 percent of all referrals came from drivers' families or friends, and 15 percent came from crash and violation record checks, courts, self-reports, and other sources. [19]

However, the assessment practices that state licensing agencies use to evaluate driver fitness are not comprehensive. For example, our review of state assessment practices indicates that all states screen for vision, but we did not find a state with screening tools to evaluate physical and cognitive functions.[20] Furthermore, the validity of assessment practices used by states is largely unknown. While research indicates that in-person license renewal is associated with lower crash rates—particularly for those aged 85 and older—other assessment practices, such as vision screening, road tests, and more frequent license renewal cycles, are not always associated with lower older driver fatality rates.[21] According to NHTSA, there is insufficient evidence on the validity and reliability of any driving assessment or screening tool. Thus, states may have difficulty discerning which tools to implement.

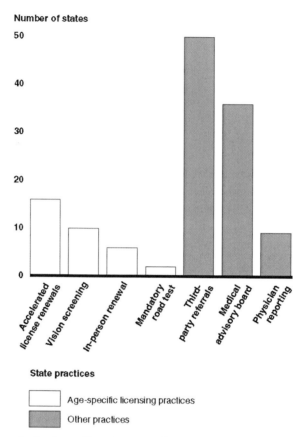

Source: GAO analysis of state licensing procedures.

Figure 12. State Licensing Practices Related to Older Driver Safety

NHTSA is Developing More Comprehensive Practices to Assess Driver Fitness

NHTSA, supported by the NIA and by partner nongovernmental organizations, has promoted research and development of mechanisms to assist licensing agencies and other stakeholders—medical providers, law enforcement officers, social service providers, family members—in better identifying medically at-risk individuals; assessing their driving fitness through a comprehensive evaluation of visual, physical, and cognitive functions; and enabling their driving for as long as safely possible. In the case of older drivers, NHTSA recognizes that only a fraction of older drivers are at increased risk of being involved in an accident and focuses its efforts on providing appropriate research-based materials and information to the broad range of stakeholders who can identify and influence the behavior of at-risk drivers.[22] Initiatives undertaken by NHTSA and its partner organizations include:

- *Model Driver Screening and Evaluation Program.* Initially developed by NHTSA in partnership with AAMVA and supported with researchers funded by NIA—the program provides a framework for driver referral, screening assessment, counseling, and licensing actions. The guidance is based on research that relates an individual's functional abilities to driving performance and reflects the results of a comprehensive research project carried out in cooperation with the Maryland Motor Vehicle Administration. Recent research supported under this program and with NIA grants evaluated a range of screenings related to visual, physical, and cognitive functions that could be completed at a licensing agency and may effectively identify drivers at an increased risk of being involved in a crash.[23]
- *Physician's Guide to Assessing and Counseling Older Drivers.* Developed by the American Medical Association to raise awareness among physicians, the guide cites relevant literature and expert views (as of May 2003) to assist physicians in judging patients' fitness to drive. The guide is based on NHTSA's earlier work with the Association for the Advancement of Automotive Medicine. This work—a detailed literature review—summarized knowledge about various categories of medical conditions, their prevalence, and their potential impact on driving ability.
- *Countermeasures That Work: A Highway Safety Countermeasure Guide for State Highway Safety Offices.* Developed with the Governors Highway Safety Association, this publication describes current initiatives in the areas of communications and outreach, licensing, and law enforcement—and the associated effectiveness, use, cost, and time required for implementation—that state agencies might consider for improving older driver safety.[24]
- *NHTSA Web site.* NHTSA maintains an older driver Web site with content for drivers, caregivers, licensing administrators, and other stakeholders to help older drivers remain safe.

- *NIA research.* NIA is supporting research on several fronts in studying risk factors for older drivers and in developing new tools for driver training and driver fitness assessment.

  - A computer-based training tool is being developed to help older drivers improve the speed with which they process visual information.[25] This tool is a self-administered interactive variation of validated training techniques that have been shown to improve visual processing speed. The tool is being designed as a cost-effective mechanism that can be broadly implemented, at social service organizations, for example, and made accessible to older drivers.

  - Driving simulators are being studied as a means of testing driving ability and retraining drivers in a manner that is more reliable and consistent than on-road testing. Virtual reality driving simulation is a potentially viable means of testing that could more accurately identify cognitive and motor impairments than could on-road tests that are comparatively less safe and more subjective.

  - Research is ongoing to evaluate the impacts of hearing loss on cognitive functions in situations, such as driving, that require multitasking.[26] Results of the research may provide insights into what level of auditory processing is needed for safe driving and may lead to development of future auditory screening tools.

  - Studies that combine a battery of cognitive function and road/driving simulator tests are being conducted to learn how age-related changes lead to hazardous driving. Results of these studies may prove useful in developing screening tests to identify functionally-impaired drivers—particularly those with dementia—who are at risk of being involved in a crash and may be unfit to drive.

NHTSA is also developing guidelines to assist states in implementing assessment practices. To date, NHTSA's research and model programs have had limited impact on state licensing practices. For example, according to NHTSA, no state has implemented the guidelines outlined in its *Model Driver Screening and Evaluation Program.* Furthermore, there is insufficient evidence on the validity and reliability of driving assessments, so states may have difficulty discerning which assessments to implement. To assist states in implementing assessment practices, NHTSA, as authorized under SAFETEA-LU section 2017, developed a plan to, among other things, (1) provide information and guidelines to people (medical providers, licensing personnel, law enforcement officers) who can influence older drivers and (2) improve the scientific basis for licensing decisions. In its plan NHTSA notes that the most important work on older driver safety that needs to occur in the next 5 years is refining screening and assessment tools and getting them into the hands of the users who need them. As an element of its plan, NHTSA is cooperating with AAMVA to create a Medical Review Task Force that will identify areas where standards of practice to assess the driving of at-risk individuals are possible and develop strategies for implementing guidelines that states can use in choosing which practices to adopt. The task force will—in areas such as vision and cognition—define existing practices used by states and identify gaps in research to encourage consensus on standards. NHTSA officials said that work is currently under way to develop neurological guidelines— which will cover issues related to cognitive assessments—and anticipate that the task force will report its findings in 2008.

SELECTED STATES HAVE IMPLEMENTED COORDINATING GROUPS AND OTHER INITIATIVES TO PROMOTE OLDER DRIVER SAFETY

Of the six states we visited, five—California, Florida, Iowa, Maryland, and Michigan— have active multidisciplinary coordination groups that may include government, medical, academic, and social service representatives, among others, to develop strategies and implement efforts to improve older driver safety.[27] Each of these states identified its coordination group as a key initiative in improving older driver safety. As shown in table 4, the coordinating groups originated in different ways and vary in size and structure. For example, Florida's At-Risk Driver Council was formally established under state legislation while Maryland's group functions on and hoc basis with no statutory authority. The approaches taken by these groups in addressing older driver safety issues vary as well. For example, California's large task force broadly reaches several state agencies and partner organizations, and the task force leaders oversee the activity of eight work groups in implementing multiple action items to improve older driver safety. In contrast, Iowa's Older Driver Target Area Team is a smaller group that operates through informal partnerships among member agencies and is currently providing consulting services to the Iowa Department of Transportation on the implementation of older driver strategies identified in Iowa's Comprehensive Highway Safety Plan.

Table 4. Older Driver Safety Coordination Groups'
Organizations and Functions

Coordinating group	Organization and function	Membership
Older Californian Traffic Safety (OCTS) Task Force	• Established in 2003 under the California Highway Patrol. • Supported by grants from California Office of Traffic Safety. • Consists of 8 work groups—(1) aging services, (2) health services, (3) law enforcement, (4) licensing, (5) mobility, (6) policy/legislation, (7) public information, (8) transportation safety—of interested stakeholders who develop and promote implementation of action items through the government agency or nongovernmental organization that they represent. • Work groups provide progress reports at quarterly OCTS Task Force meetings.	43 members that represent • state agencies, • federal agencies, • higher education institutions, • medical professional organizations, and • senior advocacy groups and service providers.
Florida At-Risk Driver Council (FADC)	• Established by state statute in 2003 and administratively supported by Department of Highway Safety and Motor Vehicles. • Chairperson elected by council members. • FADC members rank issues and establish action items in four areas: (1) prevention, early recognition, and education of at-risk drivers; (2) assessments; (3) remediation, rehabilitation, and adaptation—community and environment; (4) alternatives and accommodations for transportation. • Stakeholders implement action items through the government agency or nongovernmental organization that they represent.	33 members that represent • state agencies, • state legislators, • higher education institutions, • medical professional organizations, and • senior advocacy groups and service providers.

Table 4. (Continued)

Coordinating group	Organization and function	Membership
Iowa Older Driver Target Area Team	• Established in 1999 and operated in various forms since then to (1) coordinate public education and outreach, (2) promote research and analysis efforts, (3) provide guidance for policy and legislative considerations, and (4) promote implementation of low cost engineering safety improvements. • Team is currently reorganizing under the Iowa Traffic Safety Alliance to assist in implementing the Iowa Comprehensive Highway Safety Plan.[a]	25 members that represent • state agencies, • FHWA, • higher education institutions, and • senior advocacy groups and service providers.
Maryland Research Consortium	• Developed in 1996 under the Motor Vehicle Administration to support the *Maryland Pilot Older Driver Study*.[b] • Established working groups in four areas—(1) identification and assessment, (2) remediation and counseling, (3) mobility options, (4) public information and education—that set goals for members to meet using resources of their respective organizations.	250 members (approximate) that represent • state agencies, • federal agencies, • higher education institutions, • senior advocacy
	• Currently operates as ad hoc group to promote collaboration among interested stakeholders. • Quarterly meetings feature expert presentations on issues such as medical care for older trauma patients and transportation alternatives for older adults.	groups and service providers, • private businesses, and • interested individuals.
Michigan Senior Mobility Work Group	• Established in 1998 by SEMCOG to conduct an elderly mobility and safety assessment and develop a statewide plan of action designed to guide state policy. • Used U.S. DOT and state funds to develop its plan, *Elderly Mobility & Safety—The Michigan Approach* (1999), which outlines recommendations in the areas of (1) traffic	23 members that represent • FHWA, • state agencies, • local agencies, and •

Table 4. (Continued)

Coordinating group	Organization and function	Membership
	engineering, (2) alternative transportation, (3) housing and land use, (4) health and medicine, (5) licensing, and (6) education and awareness. • Senior Mobility Work Group has continued to update this plan—that forms the basis for strategy defined in Michigan's SHSP to address older drivers' mobility and safety—in an advisory capacity to the Governor's Traffic Safety Advisory Commission.	• senior advocacy groups and service providers.

Source: GAO.

[a] The Iowa Comprehensive Highway Safety Plan is the state's SHSP.

[b] This study was conducted under NHTSA's *Model Driver Screening and Evaluation Program.*

Members of the coordination groups we spoke with said that their state could benefit from information about other states' practices. For example, coordinating group members told us that sharing information about leading road design and licensing practices, legislative initiatives, research efforts, and model training programs that affect older drivers could support decisions about whether to implement new practices. Furthermore, group members said that identifying the research basis for practices could help them assess the benefits to be derived from implementing a particular practice. While some mechanisms exist to facilitate information exchanges on some topics, such as driver fitness assessment and licensing through AAMVA's Web site, there is no mechanism for states to share information on the broad range of efforts related to older driver safety.

In addition to coordinating groups, the six states have ongoing efforts to improve older driver safety in the areas of strategic planning, education and awareness, licensing and driver fitness assessment, engineering, and data analysis. The following examples highlight specific initiatives and leading practices in each of these categories.

Strategic planning—Planning documents establish recommended actions and provide guidance to stakeholders on ways to improve older driver safety.

- The *Michigan Senior Mobility Action Plan*, issued in November 2006, builds upon the state's 1999 plan (*Elderly Mobility & Safety—The Michigan Approach*) and outlines additional strategies, discusses accomplishments, and sets action plans in the areas of planning, research, education and awareness, engineering countermeasures, alternative transportation, housing and land use, and licensing designed to (1) reduce the number and severity of crashes involving older drivers and pedestrians, (2) increase the scope and effectiveness of alternative transportation options available to older people, (3) assist older people in maintaining mobility safely for as long as possible, and (4) plan for a day when driving may no longer be possible. In implementing this plan, officials are exploring the development of a community-based resource center that seniors can use to find information on mobility at a local level.

- *Traffic Safety among Older Adults: Recommendations for California*—developed through a grant from California's Office of Traffic Safety and published in August 2002—offers a comprehensive set of recommendations and provides guidance to help agencies and communities reduce traffic-related injuries and fatalities to older adults. The Older Californian Traffic Safety Task Force was subsequently established to coordinate the implementation of the report's recommendations.

Education/awareness—Education and public awareness initiatives enable outreach to stakeholders interested in promoting older driver safety.

- Florida GrandDriver®—based on a program developed by AAMVA— takes a multifaceted approach to public outreach through actions such as providing Web-based information related to driver safety courses and alternative transportation; training medical, social service and transportation professionals; offering safety talks at senior centers; and sponsoring CarFit events.[28] According to the Florida Department of Highway Safety and Motor Vehicles, a total of 75 training programs and outreach events were conducted under the GrandDriver program between 2000 and 2006.

- California—through its Older Californian Traffic Safety Task Force—annually holds a "Senior Safe Mobility Summit" that brings subject-matter experts and recognized leaders together to discuss issues and heighten public understanding of long-term commitments needed to help older adults drive safely longer.

Assessment/licensing—Assessment and licensing initiatives are concerned with developing better means for stakeholders—license administrators, medical professionals, law enforcement officers, family members—to determine driver fitness and provide remedial assistance to help older people remain safe while driving.

- California's Department of Motor Vehicles is continuing to develop a progressive "three-tier" system for determining drivers' wellness—through nondriving assessments in the first two tiers—and estimating driving fitness in a third-tier road test designed to assess the driver's ability to compensate for driving-relevant functional limitations identified in the first two tiers.[29] The system, currently being tested at limited locations, is being developed to keep people driving safely for as long as possible by providing a basis for a conditional licensing program that can aid drivers in improving their driving-relevant functioning and in adequately compensating for their limitations.

- Oregon requires physicians and other designated medical providers to report drivers with severe and uncontrollable cognitive or functional impairments that affect the person's ability to drive safely. Oregon Driver and Motor Vehicle Services (ODMVS) evaluates each report and determines if immediate suspension of driving privileges is necessary. A person whose driving privileges have been suspended needs to obtain medical clearance and pass ODMVS vision, knowledge, and road tests in order to have his or her driving privileges reinstated. In cases where driving privileges are not immediately suspended, people will normally be given between 30 and 60 days to pass ODMVS tests or provide medical evidence indicating that the reported condition does not present a risk to their safe driving.

- Maryland was the first state to establish a Medical Advisory Board (MAB)—created by state legislation in 1947—which is currently one of the most active boards in the United States. Maryland's MAB manages approximately 6000 cases per year—most involving older drivers. Drivers are referred from a number of sources—including physicians, law enforcement officers, friends, and relatives—and the MAB reviews screening results, physician reports, and driving records among other information to determine driving fitness. The MAB's opinion is then considered by Maryland's Motor Vehicle Administration in making licensing decisions.

- The Iowa Department of Motor Vehicles can issue older drivers restricted licenses that limit driving to daylight hours, specific geographic areas, or low-speed roads. Restricted licensing, also referred to as "graduated de-licensing," seeks to preserve the driver's mobility while protecting the health of the driver, passengers, and others on the road by limiting driving to low risk situations. About 9,000 older drivers in Iowa have restricted licenses. Iowa license examiners may travel to test older drivers in their home towns, where they feel most comfortable driving.

Engineering—Road design elements such as those recommended by FHWA are implemented to provide a driving environment that accommodates older drivers' needs.

- A demonstration program in Michigan, funded through state, county, and local government agencies, along with AAA Michigan, made low- cost improvements at over 300 high-risk, urban, signalized intersections in the Detroit area. An evaluation of 30 of these intersections indicated that the injury rate for older drivers was reduced by more than twice as much as for drivers aged 25 to 64 years.[30] The next phase of the program is development of a municipal tool kit for intersection safety, for use by municipal leaders and planners, to provide a template for implementing needed changes within their jurisdictions.
- The Iowa Department of Transportation (IDOT) has undertaken several initiatives in road operations, maintenance, and new construction to enhance the driving environment for older drivers. Among its several initiatives, IDOT is
  - using more durable pavement markings on selected roads and servicing all pavement markings on a performance-based schedule to maintain their brightness,[31]
  - adding paved shoulders with the edge line painted in a shoulder rumble strip to increase visibility and alert drivers when their vehicles stray from the travel lane,
  - converting 4-lane undivided roads to 3-lane roads with a dedicated left-turn lane to simplify turning movements,[32]

- encouraging the use of more dedicated left turn indications (arrows) on traffic signals on high-speed roads,
- installing larger street name signs,
- replacing warning signs with ones that have a fluorescent yellow background to increase visibility,
- converting to Clearview fonts[33] on Interstate signs for increased sign readability,
- demonstrating older driver and pedestrian-friendly enhancements on a roadway corridor in Des Moines, and
- promoting local implementation of roadway improvements to benefit older drivers by providing training to city and county engineers and planners.

- The Transportation Safety Work Group of the Older Californian Traffic Safety Task Force provided engineering support in updating California's highway design and traffic control manuals to incorporate FHWA's recommended practices for making travel safer and easier for older drivers. Technical experts from the work group coordinated with the Caltrans design office in reviewing the Caltrans *Highway Design Manual* and updating elements related to older driver safety. Additionally, the work group managed an expedited process to have the California Traffic Control Devices Committee consider and approve modifications to signing and pavement marking standards in the California *Manual on Uniform Traffic Control Devices* that benefit older drivers.

Data analysis—Developing tools to accurately capture accident data enables trends to be identified and resources to be directed to remediating problems.

- Iowa has a comprehensive data system that connects information from multiple sources, including law enforcement records (crash reports, traffic citations, truck inspection records) and driver license and registration databases, and can be easily accessed. For example, the system allows law enforcement officers to electronically access a person's driving record and license information at a crash scene and enter their crash reports into the data system on-scene. Data captured through this process—including the location of all crashes—is less prone to error and can be geographically referenced to identify safety issues. In the case of older driver safety, several universities are utilizing Iowa crash data in research efforts. For example, University of Northern Iowa researchers utilized crash data and geospatial analysis to demonstrate how older driver crash locations could be identified and how roadway elements could be subsequently modified to improve safety for older drivers.[34] University of Iowa researchers have used the data in behavioral research to study actions of older drivers and learn where changes in roadway geometrics, signing, or other roadway elements could assist older drivers with their driving tasks. Also, Iowa State University's Center for Transportation Research and Education (CTRE) has used the data to study a number of older driver crash characteristics and supports other older driver data analysis research projects with the Iowa Traffic Safety Data Service.[35]

- Florida is developing a Mature Driver Database (MDDB) that will collect several types of data—vision renewal data, crash data, medical review data—to be accessible through the Department of Highway Safety and Motor Vehicles (DHSMV) Web site. According to DHSMV officials, this database is intended to be used across agencies to facilitate strategic planning. DHSMV may use the database, for example, to track driver performance on screenings and analyze the effectiveness of screening methods. Planned MDDB enhancements include providing links to additional data sources such as census and insurance databases.

CONCLUSION

Older driver safety is not a high-priority issue in most states and, therefore, receives fewer resources than other safety concerns. However, the aging of the American population suggests that older driver safety issues will become more prominent in the future. Some states—with federal support— have adopted practices to improve the driving environment for older road users and have implemented assessment practices to support licensing requirements for older drivers that are more stringent than requirements for younger drivers. However, information on the effectiveness of these practices is limited, and states have been reluctant to commit resources to initiatives whose effectiveness has not been clearly demonstrated. Some states have also implemented additional initiatives to improve older driver safety, such as establishing coordination groups involving a broad range of stakeholders and developing initiatives in the areas of strategic planning, education and outreach, assessment and licensing practices, engineering, and data analysis. NHTSA and FHWA also have important roles to play in promoting older driver safety, including conducting and supporting research on standards for the driving environment and on driver fitness assessment. While states hold differing views on the importance of older driver safety and have adopted varying practices to address older driver safety issues, it is clear that there are steps that states can take to prepare for the anticipated increase in the older driver population and simultaneously improve safety for all drivers. However, state resources are limited, so information on other states' initiatives or federal efforts to develop standards for the driving environment and on driver fitness assessment practices could assist states in implementing improvements for older driver safety.

Recommendation for Executive Action

To help states prepare for the substantial increase in the number of older drivers in the coming years, we recommend that the Secretary of Transportation direct the FHWA and NHTSA Administrators to implement a mechanism that would allow states to share information on leading practices for enhancing the safety of older drivers. This mechanism could also include information on other initiatives and guidance, such as FHWA's research on the effectiveness of road design practices and NHTSA's research on the effectiveness of driver fitness assessment practices.

APPENDIX I. OBJECTIVES, SCOPE, AND METHODOLOGY

This report addresses (1) what the federal government has done to promote practices to make roads safer for older drivers and the extent to which states have implemented those practices, (2) the extent to which states assess the fitness of older drivers and what support the federal government has provided, and (3) what initiatives selected states have implemented to improve the safety of older drivers.

To determine what the federal government has done to promote practices to make roads safer for older drivers, we interviewed officials from the Federal

Highway Administration (FHWA) within the U.S. Department of Transportation (DOT) and the American Association of State and Highway Transportation Officials (AASHTO) and reviewed manuals and other documentation to determine what road design standards and guidelines have been established, the basis for their establishment, and how they have been promoted. We also reviewed research and interviewed a representative of the National Cooperative Highway Research Program (NCHRP) to gain perspective on federal initiatives to improve the driving environment for older drivers. Finally, to determine trends in accidents involving older drivers, we reviewed and analyzed crash data from the U.S. DOT's Fatality Analysis Reporting System database and General Estimates System database.

To obtain information on the extent to which states are implementing these practices, we surveyed and received responses from DOTs in each of the 50 states and the District of Columbia. We consulted with NCHRP, FHWA, and AASHTO in developing the survey. The survey was conducted from the end of September 2006 through mid-January 2007. During this time period, we sent two waves of follow-up questionnaires to nonrespondents in addition to the initial mailing. We also made phone calls and sent e-mails to a few states to remind them to return the questionnaire. We surveyed state DOTs to learn the extent to which they have incorporated federal government recommendations on road design elements into their own design guides and implemented selected recommendations in their construction, operations, and maintenance activities. We also identified reasons for state DOTs rejecting recommendations and determined the proportion of practitioners that were trained in each state to implement recommendations. In addition, we asked state DOTs to evaluate the extent to which they have developed plans (defined in Strategic Highway Safety Plans) and programmed projects (listed in Statewide Transportation Improvement Programs) for older driver safety as provided for by SAFETEA-LU legislation.

Before fielding the questionnaire, we reviewed the Safe, Accountable, Flexible, Efficient Transportation Equity Act: A Legacy for Users (SAFETEA-LU) and prior highway legislation to identify the framework for states to develop and implement older driver safety programs. Additionally, we conducted separate in-person pretests with officials from three state DOTs and revised our instrument as a result of the information obtained during those pretests. We took steps in developing the questionnaire and in collecting and analyzing the data to minimize errors that could occur during those stages of the survey process. A copy of the questionnaire and detailed survey results are available at www.gao.gov/cgi-bin/getrpt?GAO07-517SP.

To determine the extent to which states assess the fitness of older drivers and what support the federal government has provided, we interviewed officials and reviewed relevant documents from the National Highway Traffic Safety Administration within the U.S. DOT, the National Institute on Aging and the Administration on Aging within the U.S. Department of Health and Human Services, and the American Association of Motor Vehicle Administrators—a nongovernmental organization that represents state driver licensing agencies. We determined the extent to which the guidelines and model programs of these agencies addressed the visual, physical, and cognitive deficits that may afflict older drivers. We also reviewed federal, state, and nongovernmental Web sites that contained information on states' older driver licensing practices and analyzed their content so that we could compare practices across states. To obtain information on the activities of partner nongovernmental organizations in researching and promoting practices to assess older driver fitness, among other initiatives, we interviewed officials from AAA, AARP, the Insurance Institute for Highway Safety, and the Governors Highway Safety Association. To learn of states' legislative initiatives concerning driver fitness assessment and licensing, we interviewed a representative of the National Conference of State Legislatures. We also interviewed officials from departments of motor vehicles in select states to report on their efforts in developing, implementing, and evaluating older driver screening and licensing programs.

To obtain information on initiatives that selected states have implemented, we conducted case studies in six states—California, Florida, Iowa, Maryland, Michigan, and Oregon—that transportation experts identified as progressive in their efforts to improve older driver safety. We chose our case study states based on input from an NCHRP report highlighting states with leading practices in the areas of: education/awareness, assessment/licensing, engineering, agency coordination, strategic planning and data analysis. We compared practices across the six states to identify common themes. We also identified and determined, to the extent possible, key practices based on our analysis.

The scope of our work focused on older driver safety. Prior GAO work addressed the associated issue of senior mobility for those who do not drive.[36] We conducted our review from April 2006 through April 2007 in accordance with generally accepted government auditing standards. We requested official comments on this report from the U.S. Department of Transportation and the U.S. Department of Health and Human Services.

APPENDIX II. STATES' LICENSING REQUIREMENTS FOR OLDER DRIVERS

Tables 5 through 7 list older driver licensing requirements in effect in certain states.

Table 5. States with Vision Testing Requirements for Older Drivers

State	Vision test and age requirements	Additional requirements
Arizona	65 and over	None
District of Columbia	70 and over	At age 70, or nearest renewal date thereafter, a vision test is required and a reaction test may be required. Applicant must provide a statement from a practicing physician certifying the applicant to be physically and mentally competent to drive. At 75 years, or nearest renewal date thereafter, and on each subsequent renewal date, the applicant may be required to also complete the written and road tests.
Florida	80 and over	Renewal applicants 80 and older must pass a vision test administered at any driver's license office or if applying for an extension by mail must pass a vision test administered by a licensed physician or optometrist.
Georgia	64 and over	None
Maine	40 and over	Vision test required at first renewal after driver reaches age 40 and at every second renewal until age 62; thereafter, at every renewal.
Maryland	40 and over	Vision test required at *every* renewal from age 40.
Oregon	50 and over	None
South Carolina	65 and over	None
Utah	65 and over	None
Virginia	80 and over	None

Source: GAO analysis of data contained in federal, state, and nongovernmental organizations' Web sites on states' older driver licensing practices.

Table 6. States with Accelerated Renewal Cycles for Older Drivers

State	Standard renewal cycle	Accelerated renewal for older drivers with relevant ages
Arizona	Expires at age 65	5 years (65 and over)
Colorado	10 years	5 years (61 and over)
Georgia	5 or 10 years (driver option)	5 years (60 and over)
Hawaii	6 years	2 years (72 and over)
Idaho	4 years or 8years (age 21-62)	4 years (63and over)
Illinois	4 years	2 years (81 to 86); 1 year (87 and over)
Indiana	4 years	3years (75 and older)
Iowa	5 years	2 years (70 and older)
Kansas	6 years	4 years (65 and older)
Maine	6 years	4 years (65 and older)
Missouri	6 years	3years (70 and older)
Montana	8years	4 years (75 and older)
New Mexico	4 years or 8years (driver option)	4 years (for drivers who would turn 75 inlast half of an 8-year cycle)
North Carolina	8years	5 years (54 and older)
Rhode Island	5 years	2 years (70 and older)
South Carolina	10 years	5 years (65 and older)

Source: GAO analysis of data contained in federal, state, and nongovernmental organizations' Web sites on states' older driver licensing practices.

Table 7. States Requiring In-Person Renewals

State	Age for in-person renewals	Additional requirements
Alaska	69 and over	Mail renewal not available to people 69 and older and to people whose prior renewal was by mail.
Arizona	70 and over	It cannot be renewed by mail.
California	70 and over	At age 70, mail renewal is prohibited. No more than two sequential mail renewals are permitted, regardless of age.
Colorado	61 and over	Mail or electronic renewal not available to people 61 and older and to people whose prior renewal was electronic or by mail.
Louisiana	70 and over	Mail renewal not available to people 70 and older and to people whose prior renewal was by mail.

Source: GAO analysis of data contained in federal, state, and nongovernmental organizations' Web sites on states' older driver licensing practices.

APPENDIX III. COMMENTS FROM DEPARTMENT OF HEALTH AND HUMAN SERVICES

DEPARTMENT OF HEALTH & HUMAN SERVICES

Office of the Assistant Secretary for Legislation

Washington, D.C. 20201

MAR 1 C 2007

Ms. Katherine Siggerud
Director, Physical Infrastructure Issues
U.S. Government Accountability Office
Washington, DC 20548

Dear Ms. Siggerud:

Enclosed are the Department's comments on the U.S. Government Accountability Office's (GAO) draft report entitled, "Older Driver Safety: Knowledge Sharing Should Help States Prepare for Increase in Older Driver Population" (GAO-07-413), before its publication.

The department appreciates the opportunity to comment on this daft report.

Sincerely,

Rebecca Kemard

Vincent J. Ventimiglia
Assistant Secretary for Legislation

GENERAL COMMENTS ON THE DEPARTMENT OF HEALTH AND HUMAN SERVICES ON THE GOVERNMENT ACCOUNTABILITY OFFICE DRAFT REPORT ENTITLED: OLDER DRIVER SAFETY: KNOWLEDGE SHARING SHOULD HELP STATES PREPARE OR INCREASE IN OLDER DRIVER POPULATION (GAO 07-413)

HHS COMMENTS

As indicated in this report, older driver safety is important now, since based on miles driven older drivers have a comparatively higher involvement in fatal crashes; and it is important for planning for the future, since by 2030 the number of licensed drivers 65 and older is estimated to nearly double.

This report provides a focus on two critical priority issues: what the states need to do to improve highway safety and adoption of screening practices for older drivers. The report covers what the federal government has done to promote older driver safety through practices related to road construction and highway signage, especially relating to intersections; and what the states have done to implement these practices and what initiatives they have undertaken either specifically targeted at older drivers or as a byproduct of safety measures for drivers of all ages. The report also provides much useful information about older driver assessment practices across a number of states.

There is a recommendation for executive action by the Secretary of Transportation to implement a mechanism to allow states to share information on leading practices for enhancing the safety of older drivers. We would also suggest that other issues to be addressed are the transition out of driving by assisting older adults with the decision to stop driving; and how communities can best provide viable alternative forms of transportation enabling older adults to maintain optimal autonomy.

This a well conceptualized and executed report on current state practices and federal initiatives which will provide a sound foundation for identifying and implementing measures that will enhance the safety of older drivers.

End Notes

[1] This report generally refers to survey responses from the 50 states and the District of Columbia as "states' responses."

[2] GAO, *Transportation Disadvantaged Seniors: Efforts to Enhance Senior Mobility Could Benefit from Additional Guidance and Information*, GAO-04-971 (Washington, D.C.: Aug. 30, 2004).

[3] Hauer, E., "The Safety of Older Persons at Intersections." *Transportation in an Aging Society*, vols. 1 and 2, Special Reports 218. Transportation Research Board. (Washington, D.C.: 1988).

[4] Pub. L. No. 109-59, 119 Stat. 1144 (2005).

[5] Section 1405 of SAFETEA-LU directs DOT to carry out a program to improve traffic signs and pavement markings to accommodate older drivers and authorizes to be appropriated such sum as may be necessary to carry out this section for the fiscal years 2005 through 2009. No funds have been specifically appropriated for this purpose, and FHWA officials indicated that they are using limited available program funds to satisfy the intent of the legislation. Section 2017 of SAFETEA-LU authorizes NHTSA's research and demonstration program.

[6] Practices are based on guidelines and recommendations published in three FHWA documents: *Highway Design Handbook for Older Drivers and Pedestrians (2001); Guidelines and Recommendations to Accommodate Older Drivers and Pedestrians (2001); and Travel Better, Travel Longer: A Pocket Guide to Improve Traffic Control and Mobility for Our Older Population* (2003). FHWA researched and developed its guidelines and recommendations in collaboration with highway engineering experts from the American Association of State Highway and Transportation Officials—a nonprofit association representing highway and transportation departments in the United States and Puerto Rico; the National Committee on Uniform Traffic Control Devices—a group that makes recommendations to FHWA on standards codified in the Manual on Uniform Traffic Control Devices; and the Transportation Research Board—a division of the National Research Council which serves as an independent adviser to the federal government to promote innovation and progress in transportation through research.

[7] FHWA issues national standards for traffic control devices in its *Manual on Uniform Traffic Control Devices* (MUTCD). States are required by federal code to adopt the federal MUTCD or adopt a state MUTCD that is in substantial compliance with FHWA's MUTCD within 2 years of FHWA issuing a new edition or revision. Of the 136 recommendations in FHWA's *Highway Design Handbook for Older Drivers and Pedestrians* (2001), 43 relate to traffic control devices and are included in the current edition (2003) of the federal MUTCD. FHWA does not issue geometric road design standards for the layout of roads. Rather, FHWA works with states and other transportation industry groups to establish national geometric road design standards, and state transportation officials then rely on those standards in developing their own road design standards.

[8] The study is being supported by funds "pooled" from multiple sources to investigate 20 selected strategies described in the National Cooperative Highway Research Program (NCHRP) Report 500 guidebooks. The NCHRP Report 500 is a series of guides being developed by the Transportation Research Board to assist state and local agencies in reducing injuries and fatalities in targeted areas, such as older drivers. Each guide includes a general description of the problem, strategies and countermeasures to address the problem, and a model implementation process; however, not all strategies in the guides have been proven through properly designed evaluations. Most roadway and engineering strategies highlighted in the NCHRP Report 500 (*Volume 9: A Guide for Reducing Collisions Involving Older Drivers*) also appear in FHWA's *Highway Design Handbook for Older Drivers and Pedestrians*. The goal of the research is to develop reliable estimates of the effectiveness of safety

improvements identified in the NCHRP Report 500 guidebooks in locations where these strategies are being implemented.

[9] SAFETEA-LU provides funding for many types of projects under programs such as the Interstate Maintenance Program, the Surface Transportation Program, and the National Highway System Program. These programs have set requirements as to the types of roads that are eligible for project funding and the purposes for which the funds can be used.

[10] SAFETEA-LU requires each state receiving funds under the HSIP to develop a SHSP that identifies safety problems and analyzes opportunities for corrective action. SHSPs are to be based on a system that collects crash data, identifies problems, and analyzes countermeasures that can be implemented. By October 1, 2006, each state was to have a strategic highway safety plan and, as of January 8, 2007, FHWA reports having received SHSPs from 28 states.

[11] Fifty states and the District of Columbia responded to the survey. One state did not respond to this question.

[12] According to FHWA Highway Statistics (2005), states own, on average, 19 percent of public roads, while local agencies own 76 percent of public roads nationwide. However, ownership varies considerably by state. For example, Iowa owns 7.8 percent of the public roads in the state, while West Virginia owns 91.8 percent.

[13] In cooperation with other units of government, each state produces a STIP that describes those projects that will be implemented over (at least) the following 4 years. The STIP includes all projects or phases of transportation project development that will use federal transportation funds and includes all regionally significant transportation projects requiring federal approval or permits (even if no federal funds are to be used in the construction). The type of information provided for each project in the STIP includes the project description, estimated cost, amount and category of federal funds to be used, amount and source of nonfederal funds to be used, and the agency responsible for project implementation.

[14] See J.T. Bruff and J. Evans, *Elderly Mobility and Safety—The Michigan Approach, Final Plan of Action*. SEMCOG. (Detroit: 1999).

[15] FHWA safety analysts have recently analyzed the results of several studies on intersection improvements implemented in Iowa, Michigan, and overseas in France. In general, FHWA found that intersection improvements have an even greater benefit, in terms of reduced crashes, for older drivers than for younger drivers.

[16] Under the HSIP in SAFETEA-LU, 21 types of projects can be funded, including safety projects for high-risk rural roads, railway/highway crossings, work zones, collection and analysis of crash data, roadside obstacle elimination, pedestrian, bicycle intersections and others. Our survey asked to what extent state DOTs had invested resources in a selection of safety projects (from the HSIP), older driver safety projects (from the Roadway Safety Improvements for Older Drivers and Pedestrians program), and projects to create safe routes to schools (from the Safe Routes to School program).

[17] To obtain information on states' licensing requirements, we reviewed federal, state, and nongovernmental Web sites that contained information on states' older driver licensing laws and analyzed their content so that we could compare practices across states.

[18] Visual acuity measures the clarity or sharpness of vision. The test for visual acuity measures how clearly a person can see from a distance, and results are expressed in a fraction such as 20/20. The top number refers to the distance the person being tested stands from the chart—usually 20 feet. The bottom number indicates the distance at which a person with normal eyesight could read the same line that the person being tested correctly read. For example, 20/20 is considered normal, and a 20/40 measure indicates that the line the person being tested correctly read at 20 feet can be read by a person with normal vision from 40 feet away.

[19] Stutts, J.C., *Improving the Safety of Older Road Users*. National Cooperative Highway Research Program Synthesis Project 20-5, Synthesis Topic 35-10. (Washington, D.C.: Transportation Research Board, 2005).

[20] All states require vision testing, and visual acuity of 20/40 or better (corrected or uncorrected) in one eye alone is typically needed in order to obtain a license.

[21] See David Grabowski, Christine Campbell, and Michael Morrisey, "Elderly Licensure Laws and Motor Vehicle Fatalities," *Journal of the American Medical Association* 291 (2004): 2,840-2,846.

[22] While outside the purview of this report, NHTSA is also conducting vehicle-related research efforts on older driver safety, including crashworthiness research to develop more effective restraints for older occupants.

[23] Karlene K.Ball et al., "Can High-Risk Older Drivers Be Identified through Performance-Based Measures in a Department of Motor Vehicles Setting?" *Journal of the American Geriatrics Society* 54 (2006): 77-84.

[24] The Governors Highway Safety Association (GHSA) is a nonprofit association representing state highway safety offices that promotes the development of policy and programs to improve traffic safety. GHSA members are appointed by their governors to administer federal and state highway safety funds and implement state highway safety plans.

[25] As people age, their speed of visual processing, or ability to recognize what they see, diminishes. Previous NIA-sponsored research shows that reduced visual processing speed—determined through a measure termed "useful field of view"—increases the crash risk for older drivers. (See Owsley, C. et al., "Visual Processing Impairment and Risk of Motor Vehicle Crash Among Older Adults," *Journal of the American Medical Association* 279, vol. 14 [1998].)

[26] Hearing impairment, common among older adults, compromises cognitive functions in that attention is diverted away from other tasks to focus on auditory processing.

[27] Oregon, the remaining state we visited, previously had an At-Risk Driver Public Education Consortium to coordinate a pubic education initiative addressing older driver safety among other issues. Consortium members represented state agencies, public transit districts, senior service providers, and other stakeholders. The consortium was disbanded in 2003.

[28] The CarFit program is designed to help mature drivers find out how well they currently fit their cars and what actions they might take to improve their fit. The program is a joint venture by the American Occupational Therapy Association, the American Society on Aging, AAA Auto Club, and AARP.

[29] The three-tier system addresses the driving-related medical problems and functional limitations that occur most often among older drivers but also occur among younger drivers. A driving wellness assessment that includes evaluation of a person's functional health relevant for driving, understanding of driving practices, and knowledge of laws and rules of the road is the focus of the first two tiers. The tiers are progressive in that a person who successfully passes the first-tier assessment and knowledge test will not be assessed further. A driving fitness assessment that evaluates how a driver actually drives with his/her functional limitations is the focus of the third tier.

[30] AAA, *Intersection Improvements Reduce Senior Driver Injuries at a Rate Much Higher Than Other Age Groups, According to AAA Study* (Washington, D.C.: 6/27/2005).

[31] Iowa based its strategy to improve pavement marking visibility on research conducted by the University of Iowa Center for Computer Aided Design, Operator Performance Laboratory. The research report "Enhancing Pavement Marking Visibility for Older Drivers" was prepared for IDOT in March 2003.

[32] Having a dedicated left-turn lane simplifies left-turn movements onto and off of the mainline. Iowa State University researchers studied 14 of these converted corridors and documented a 24 percent reduction in the crash rate for all drivers and a 28 percent reduction in the crash rate for drivers aged 65 and older.

[33] FHWA has given interim approval for states to use Clearview font legends (lettering) on guide signs. Clearview fonts were designed to make highway signs easier for older drivers to read without having to increase letter height or sign size.

[34] Strauss, Tim and Elder, Jess, "Crash Patterns of Older Drivers in Iowa: A Systematic Spatial Analysis," University of Northern Iowa, July 2004. This report was funded by the Iowa Department of Transportation.

[35] The Iowa Traffic Safety Data Service is a program of the CTRE that produces crash data analyses for use by traffic engineers, researchers, law enforcement officials, and others who need the information for purposes such as making funding decisions, developing road improvement projects, and implementing enforcement actions.

[36] GAO-04-971.

CHAPTER SOURCES

The following chapters have been previously published:

Chapter 1 – This is an edited, reformatted and augmented version of a United States Department of Transportation, National Highway Traffic Safety Administration publication.

Chapter 2 - This is an edited, reformatted and augmented version of a United States Government Accountability Office publication, Report GAO-07-413, dated April 2007.

INDEX

collaboration, 99, 112
collisions, 8, 18, 31, 40, 46, 49
community, 80, 98, 101
compliance, 112
computer, 96
configuration, 49
conformity, 54
consciousness, 93
consensus, 75, 97
construction, 70, 80, 81, 84, 86, 87, 90, 103, 107, 113
consulting, 97
contributing factors, 2, 6, 7, 9, 10, 12, 41
control measures, 8
cooperation, 95, 113
coordination, 71, 75, 88, 97, 100, 106, 108
cost, 75, 81, 84, 95, 96, 99, 103, 113
counsel, 54
counseling, 95, 99
crash involvement ratio (CIR), vii, 1, 3, 5, 12
cycles, 74, 92, 93

D

data analysis, 8, 9, 10, 71, 75, 100, 105, 106, 108
data set, 5
database, 9, 41, 52, 105, 107
datasets, 48
dementia, 76, 93, 96
demographic change, 13
Department of Health and Human Services, 70, 73, 76, 108, 111
Department of Transportation (DOT), viii, 67, 69, 70, 71, 73, 76, 80, 83, 85, 87, 89, 90, 97, 99, 103, 107, 108, 112, 115, 117
depth, vii, 1, 5, 33
derivatives, 14, 35
designers, 80
diagnosis, 93
distribution, 6, 11

District of Columbia, 73, 74, 92, 107, 109, 112, 113
doctors, 93
draft, 76
drugs, 10, 20, 21, 40, 41, 55

E

education, 71, 75, 80, 90, 98, 99, 100, 101, 106, 108, 114
e-mail, 107
emergency, 54
enforcement, 80, 93, 94, 95, 97, 98, 102, 104, 115
engineering, 71, 75, 80, 90, 99, 100, 101, 104, 106, 108, 112
environment, 3, 98, 103, 105, 107
environmental characteristics, vii, 1, 4, 16, 38
environmental conditions, 52
epilepsy, 93
equipment, 9
evidence, 53, 75, 87, 92, 93, 96, 102
examinations, 92
executive function, 54
exposure, vii, 1, 2, 3, 5, 6, 8, 10, 11, 12, 13, 21, 22, 25, 30, 33, 37, 38, 41, 52, 54, 66
exposure analyses, 2, 3, 8, 10, 21

F

families, 93
family members, 80, 94, 102
Fatality Analysis Reporting System (FARS), vii, 1, 4
fear, 93
federal funds, 113
federal government, viii, 69, 72, 73, 106, 107, 108, 112
Federal Highway Administration (FHWA), 70, 71, 73, 74, 76, 78, 80, 81, 83, 84, 85,

S

T

-07-517SP